The Archaeology of Old Nuulliit

MONOGRAPHS ON GREENLAND
Vol. 349

MAN & SOCIETY
Vol. 39

Mikkel Sørensen

The Archaeology of Old Nuulliit

Eigil Knuth's Investigations in the Thule Region,
North Greenland, 1952–1990

MUSEUM TUSCULANUM PRESS
UNIVERSITY OF COPENHAGEN
2010

Mikkel Sørensen
The Archaeology of Old Nuulliit: Eigil Knuth's Investigations in the Thule Region, North Greenland, 1952–1990

© Museum Tusculanum Press and the author, 2010
Consultants: Claus Andreasen and Pierre M. Desrosiers
Layout, composition and cover design: Erling Lynder
Printed in Denmark by Special-Trykkeriet Viborg a-s
ISBN 978 87 635 3166 5

Monographs on Greenland | Meddelelser om Grønland, vol. 349
ISSN 0025 6676

Man & Society, vol. 39
ISSN 0106 1062
Series editor: Hans Christian Gulløv

www.mtp.dk/MoG

Front cover images: Air photo of the Nuulliit peninsula (Photo E. Knuth) and lithic harpoon point of Late Dorset type from the H-plateau at Nuulliit (Drawing H.C. Gulløv)

Back cover image: The camp of E. Hoffmeyer and E. Knuth at Nuulliit during the 1975 season (Photo E. Knuth)

This book is published with financial support from
The Peary Land Foundation

Museum Tusculanum Press
126 Njalsgade
DK-2300 Copenhagen S
Denmark
www.mtp.dk

Foreword

'This book and the entire material from Old Nuulliit are willed to Bjarne Grønnow'. The text is written on a label glued to the back of one of Eigil Knuth's ring binders containing drawings, photos, lists and bits and pieces of manuscripts from his investigations at Old Nuulliit in the Thule area. Discovering this message from Eigil Knuth, among dozens of binders, folders and portfolios kept in the Queen's Personal Library in the cellars of the royal castle of Amalienborg, touched me deeply and encouraged me to initiate the process that has led to the present publication.

When I published the book *The Northernmost Ruins of the Globe* with Ph.D. Jens Fog Jensen in 2003, celebrating the 100th birthday of the late Count Eigil Knuth (1903–1996), we presented the archaeological sites that, throughout six decades of exploration and research activities in High Arctic Greenland, he had surveyed and investigated but only sporadically published. The information from these Palaeo-Eskimo and Thule Culture sites was comprehensive, and we had to restrict the book to cover sites from Washington Land via Peary Land to North East Greenland, i.e. the sites along the 'Musk Ox Way'. Thus, the archival material and artefact assemblage from the important and complex site of Old Nuulliit in the Thule Area – part of the southbound 'Caribou Way' – was deliberately omitted and left for future analyses.

Fortunately, this was not a distant future: in 2005 the Peary Land Foundation and SILA (the Greenland Research Centre at the National Museum of Denmark) joined forces on a publication project on Old Nuulliit. Consequently, Postdoctoral Fellow Mikkel Sørensen became involved in the project. He was a perfect choice for the task, but before I elaborate on that, I must briefly return to events some 30 years ago.

Old Nuulliit was on the agenda from the very first time that I, as a young student in 1978, visited Eigil Knuth in his studio apartment on the fourth floor in Carl Johans Gade in Copenhagen. The assemblage was his favourite as well as his problem child. It did not fit into his Independence Culture concept. According to a couple of ^{14}C datings, the site was the earliest in the entire Eastern Arctic, and this was, in Eigil Knuth's opinion, in accordance with the few but quite remarkable artefacts, which he had found during his early investigations: i.e. a tiny arrow point and a huge 'stone wedge'. Eigil Knuth kept the small assemblage from Old

Nuulliit in a cupboard in his bedroom, everything carefully numbered and stored in small boxes. Regularly, when I visited him during the next 15 years, he would fetch these finds and bring them into the light at his heavily loaded desk. Holding the arrow point or a knife blade under his magnifying glass he would elaborate on the technical competence of his 'Old Nuulliit Culture' and discuss with me equivalent Saqqaq artefacts from West Greenland, which of course did not achieve the technical and design standards of the 'Old Nuulliit Culture'.

Little did I know that by expressing my doubt of the validity of the ^{14}C datings, which were based on bones from marine mammals and reached back into the 5th millennium BC, I contributed to a process that menaced our friendship – he sometimes called me day and night to blame me and other archaeologists for their distrust in his work – and in the end almost became the death of him: In 1990, at the age of 87, Eigil Knuth used his last economic, psychological and physical resources to head an expedition to Old Nuulliit in order to finally settle matters and prove that he was right about the age of the culture. Considering the circumstances, Eigil Knuths's two students did a marvellous job excavating and surveying a number of features at Old Nuulliit, but from the entries in his diary – brief sentences written with a trembling hand – you can tell that, during the 1990 season, he really suffered severely from the cold and from illness in this forbidding peninsula. On top of that he was disappointed about the results of the field work – no finds of organic materials or substantial lithic artefact assemblages were brought home from Old Nuulliit. However, the information from this, his very last excavation in the High Arctic, is a key to a new interpretation of the cultural chronology and history of the site.

As mentioned above, Eigil Knuth, to my surprise, emphasized in his will that the rights to the Old Nuullit archive were granted to me. I interpreted this as the right to carry out a publication project on this material. As an in-depth analysis of the lithics of Old Nuulliit was essential to a re-interpretation of the site, the choice of an expert to carry out the task was straightforward. I appointed Mikkel Sørensen, who had just finished his Ph.D. dissertation on Palaeo-Eskimo lithic assemblages from Greenland based on dynamic technological analyses. Subsequently, the Peary Land Foundation and SILA agreed on funding the publication process.

Mikkel Sørensen has worked professionally and intensively with the archival as well as the lithic material from the site and he has succeeded in bringing the complex Old Nuulliit site into a new meaningful context. Eigil Knuth was right: Old Nuulliit certainly is a key site to the understanding of the very early cultural history of Greenland; but, as Mikkel's analyses show, in quite another way than Eigil Knuth imagined. In my opinion, Mikkel successfully demonstrates in this book that Eigil Knuth's work at Old Nuulliit represents a most important scientific achievement, while at the same time there is room for new interpretation. Thus, the present publication is in accordance with and should be seen as a continuation of *The Northernmost Ruins of the Globe* from 2003.

I wish to extend my thanks to the board of the Peary Land Foundation, who has supported the publication project of Old Nuulliit in every respect. Ph.D. Aoife Daly is thanked for translation and linguistic revision. Our colleagues at the SILA centre were, as they always are, brilliant discussants during the work process. Finally, I wish to warmly thank Mikkel Sørensen for his commitment and professionalism and congratulate him on this important re-interpretation of the Old Nuulliit site.

Bjarne Grønnow, SILA – The Greenland Research
Centre at the National Museum of Denmark
Gershøj, 17 December 2007

Contents

Foreword 5
Acknowledgements 11

1.0 The field of research 13

1.1 Eigil Knuth and Nuulliit 13
1.1.1 Eigil Knuth's work and problems with the Nuulliit material 13
1.1.2 Eigil Knuth's motivation for surveying the Thule region 15
1.1.3 Previous work from the Thule region that inspired Eigil Knuth 17
1.1.4 Eigil Knuth's introduction to the archaeology at Nuulliit 18
1.1.5 Eigil Knuth's four seasons at Nuulliit 21
1.1.6 How artefacts and documentation from Nuulliit were re-investigated and a new interpretation of the prehistory at Nuulliit emerged 27

1.2 The environment at Nuulliit 30
1.2.1 Environmental preconditions for a hunter-gatherer society at Nuulliit: the sea-ice situation 30
1.2.2 The climate in the prehistoric period 34
1.2.3 Marine and terrestrial resources in the Nuulliit area 35
1.2.4 Geography and landscape 38
1.2.5 Geology and geological resources 39

1.3 Eigil Knuth's first surveys to find Palaeo-Eskimos in the Thule region, 1952–1958 41

1.4 The Archaeology of New Nuulliit 49
1.4.1 New Nuulliit: Holtved's investigations 49
1.4.2 Eigil Knuth's excavations of Thule culture ruins at 'New Nuulliit' ... 50

2.0 The Archaeology of Old Nuulliit

2.1 Eigil Knuth's investigations of Old Nuulliit: ruins, artefacts and prehistoric traditions for each plateau

2.1.1 Terminology and landscape 54
2.1.2 The A-plateau 58
2.1.3 The B-plateau 73
2.1.4 The C-plateau 76
2.1.5 The D-plateau 87
2.1.6 The E-plateau 93
2.1.7 The F-plateau 96
2.1.8 The H-plateau 117
2.1.9 The I-area 126

2.2 Organic material from Old Nuulliit 127

2.3 Absolute dating 129

2.4 Later archaeological investigations at Nuulliit 131

3.0 Discussion 132

3.1 The settlements at Old Nuulliit and their cultural affiliations 132

3.2 Eigil Knuth as an archaeologist at Nuulliit 138

3.3 Conclusions 139

4.0 Perspectives and potentials: Nuulliit and the archaeology of the Thule region 140

Appendix: List of place names and terminology 142
Bibliography 143

Acknowledgements

This monograph is based on a postdoctoral project funded by the Peary Land Foundation and SILA – The Greenland Research Centre at the National Museum of Denmark. I warmly thank these two organizations and the heir of the rights to access Eigil Knuth's archaeological archive, Research Professor Bjarne Grønnow, for giving me the opportunity to work with Eigil Knuth's unique materials. The project was carried out at SILA in the period 2006–07, in the wake of my Ph.D. project, *Technology and Tradition in the Eastern Arctic from 2500 BC to 1200 AD*, which was hosted by SILA as well. The daily interactions with my colleagues at SILA and its many guest researchers have been extremely important to my work on many levels and have contributed to a most fruitful process. Thus, I extend my warmest thanks to all my colleagues, with whom I have discussed problems and potentials of the Old Nuulliit material.

I would also like to express my gratitude to the staff at the Ethnographic Collections for patiently assisting me with locating the artefacts. I am grateful to the Queen's Library at Amalienborg for facilitating my work with the Knuth Archive. Important comments to the text were given by Claus Andreasen (The Greenland National Museum and Archive) and Pierre Desrosiers (Avataq Cultural Institute), who took the time to carefully read through the manuscript. Aoife Daly skilfully translated Eigil Knuth's text and proofread mine. I thank her for flexibility and professionalism in connection with this process. I would also like to thank photographer Jeppe Sørensen for his photographs of the lithic material. This was not an easy task, but he solved it beautifully. Finally I would like to thank Museum Tusculanum Press for ensuring the continuous publication of Monographs on Greenland and for maintaining the high quality of the series.

Mikkel Sørensen

1.0 The field of research

1.1 Eigil Knuth and Nuulliit

1.1.1 Eigil Knuth's work and problems with the Nuulliit material

Nuulliit was certainly never an easy project for Eigil Knuth, although since its discovery it was always one of his 'crown jewels'. In this publication, the story about Knuth's discovery of Nuulliit is told. What can we learn from Knuth's excavations on Nuulliit and from his following reflections and interpretations? Moreover, the publication presents all the different records and descriptions which Knuth himself already had produced for a final Nuulliit volume, but never managed to publish.

Eigil Knuth was, without a doubt, a pioneer in archaeology, certainly in Northeast Greenland where he, as the first archaeologist, proved the existence of two Palaeo-Eskimo migrations. However, it is less known that he was a pioneer, as well, in the Thule region and on Ellesmere Island. To be a pioneer like Eigil Knuth in his field is magnificent and glorious, but it is also problematic, not least on a scientific level. All the observations you make in a completely new field, in archaeology, as well as in any other science, are logically unknown, and have to be reported, defined, named and interpreted for the first time. In the Thule region, the only archaeologists Knuth could refer to were Erik Holtved and George Comer. However these two persons were mainly engaged with the Thule culture. Moreover, the Thule region has, since Knuth's time, unveiled itself as the most culturally complex area of Greenland, including no less than six different Palaeo-Eskimo cultural traditions (Grønnow and Sørensen 2006, Sørensen 2006a and Sørensen 2010) and several Thule Culture migrations. To put it briefly: in a modern perspective, it is not strange that Nuulliit, archaeologically, was a difficult project for Eigil Knuth.

Eigil Knuth's field notes, photographs, drawings, plans, diaries and manuscripts about Nuulliit, by will, were left to Bjarne Grønnow and entrusted to her Majesty the Queen's Royal Library, where the material is stored today. Eigil Knuth was extremely serious about his work, and not least about what should happen with his field notes, manuscripts and records after his time. When Bjarne and I arrived at the Queen's library we discovered that there existed a file containing a manuscript about the Nuulliit material (Knuth 1977). On this file, Knuth's characteristic handwriting stated "Testamenteret Bjarne Grønnow" (Left by will to Bjarne Grønnow). Thus it was Knuth's will that Bjarne should be the one who finally published Nuulliit. Today Bjarne is head of SILA, the Greenlandic Research Centre at the National Museum. Acknowledging that he could not find coherent time to analyse and publish Eigil Knuth's material due to administrative obligations, Bjarne raised funding from the Peary Land Foundation for the project, and I was employed at SILA to complete the project. However, Bjarne has been an important partner and discussant all the way through the project. Today we both feel that Eigil Knuth would be satisfied with this publication and reinterpretation of Nuulliit, even though he might be critical (not to say angry) that someone would dare to comment on his work.

As mentioned, Eigil Knuth had been working intensively with a manuscript about the archaeology of Nuulliit. Handwritten comments on some of the pages showed that a monograph in *Meddelelser om Grønland* was planned. Parts of the manuscript were dated to 1977, and thus contained material from his three first campaigns at Nuulliit (1958, 1960, 1975). Knuth did publish some of his main thoughts about Nuulliit in both English and Danish, in journals (Knuth 1977/78; Knuth 1978), but the monograph was never produced. Today, when reading his unpublished manuscripts, some of the reasons why it was never published become clear. The site of Nuulliit was complex in respect to its internal organization and in relation to several cultural characteristics. Moreover, Eigil Knuth changed his mind about essential interpretations, as time went on, and new journeys were made to Nuulliit. In his first interpretations Knuth believed that the site yielded three ruin groups (like Holtved had described from the Thule Culture at New Nuulliit), so that there were three ruin groups on both Old Nuulliit and New Nuulliit (Eigil Knuth's terminology). Moreover, he believed that the three ruin groups at Old Nuulliit were identical to three different Palaeo-Eskimo migrations and traditions (Knuth 1977/78, 1978). However he discarded this terminology and idea and started to describe the ruins according to their positions on the many different plateaus. This was a less constructed and more realistic terminology and interpretation, still used in this publication.

In the use of radiocarbon dating also, Eigil Knuth was a pioneer. He collaborated with one of the first radiocarbon laboratories, which was situated at the National Museum of Denmark. However, radiocarbon dating was not an easy task at Nuulliit. The only organic material he could find at Nuulliit in association with the ruins, that was large enough for conventional dating, was bone from marine mammals. Thus dates of the ruins became unreliable, a fact that he gradually had to face while trying to understand the chronology at Nuulliit and finish his manuscript. Knuth's last season at Nuulliit, during 1990, while he was 87 years old, has to be seen in this light. Knuth *had* to go back in order to provide terrestrial bone material or charcoal made from local wood, to achieve some convincing absolute dating which would confirm his interpretations.

1.1.2 Eigil Knuth's motivation for surveying the Thule region

Eigil Knuth was the first person to start surveying systematically for Palaeo-Eskimo settlement in the Thule region. From 1947, the first sites containing evidence of a Stone Age in Greenland were discovered (Jensen 2003). In eastern North Greenland, Eigil Knuth found what he later termed the Independence I and Independence II cultures. Meanwhile, in West Greenland, Meldgaard and others documented the existence of Palaeo-Eskimo sites, later termed Saqqaq and Dorset. Moreover, in 1948 Helge Larsen and Erik Holtved met with Louis Giddings in Alaska and were presented to the 'Palaeolithic' collection from Cape Denbigh in Alaska. They recognized that the same type of artefacts were found in Greenland, and could conclude that Greenland had a previously unacknowledged Stone Age. Thus, Giddings's excavations at Cape Denbigh and his later publications (1964) had major influence for the definition and understanding of the 'Palaeolithic' artefacts found in Greenland, and one can say especially for Knuth's perception of 'Old Nuulliit'.

The Stone Age of Greenland was finally acknowledged when Meldgaard, in 1952, and Knuth, in 1952, published their articles, respectively, about lithic burins in Disco Bay (Meldgaard 1952) and the archaeology of Peary Land (Knuth 1952).

The early explorations of the first migrations into Greenland were influenced by ethnographic theories (Steensby 1910) and a few observations, from early expeditions, of structures belonging to the Thule Culture (e.g. Rasmussen 1919). Especially Steensby's theory, describing a 'musk ox way' north of Greenland and a 'reindeer way' through West Greenland, was adapted by Eigil Knuth as an important part of his conception of the prehistory of Greenland. Knuth explained his discoveries of early Palaeo-Eskimo presence in Peary Land (the Independence Culture) as a result of migrating people following the musk ox north of Greenland. Conversely, and in accordance with the theory of Steensby, he perceived early human remains in the Thule region as evidence of people migrating along 'the reindeer way'. One could therefore say that a prime motivation for Knuth surveying the Thule region was to 'document' the reindeer way as formulated by Steensby. He was in this respect well aware that the first migrations into West Greenland would have been through the Thule region, as he doubted that the Independence I went around Greenland and into Disco Bay (figure 1.1).

Moreover, Eigil Knuth suggested that at least two more prehistoric migrations

THE FIELD OF RESEARCH

1.1
The Eastern Arctic

came through North Greenland. To argue for this idea he pointed out the existence of two types of so called 'shelter ruins' found in Northeast Greenland, originally defined by Bendix Thostrup during the Denmark Expedition (Thostrup 1911). One of the shelter ruin types Knuth described relates to the Thule culture, while he kept it an open question as to which culture used the second type (in his manuscript from 1977). Probably Knuth suspected that the other type was a remnant of a third Palaeo-Eskimo migration: a third Independence culture! As we shall see in Knuth's descriptions and excavations of shelter-like structures at Nuulliit, he was, during his first seasons, searching persistently for attributes related to Palaeo-Eskimo cultures in shelter ruins, possibly because finds of early inventory would enable him to identify a third Independence culture. In relation to this, Eigil Knuth found the following statement of Holtved, concerning Holtved's excavations of the ruin group III of Thule houses at Nuulliit, of great interest: 'Unfortunately lack of time made it impossible to excavate them [shelter ruins nos. 47, 48 in group III]. It should be done in the future, as no doubt they belong to the oldest habitation of Nûgdlît' (Holtved 1954: 10). This statement provided Knuth with an important argument to go to Nuulliit in 1958. Eigil Knuth wrote about Holtved's statement:

This cited remark made it the natural choice that, at my arrival at the site in 1958, where my precise purpose was to identify traces of early cultures, I should begin the work by subjecting New Nûgdlît's ruin group III to examination (Knuth 1997).

He arrived at a conclusion concerning shelter ruins and the Palaeo-Eskimos, terming this phase a Meso-Eskimo site (Knuth 1977/78), but he was never so certain that he dared publish his idea about the third Independence culture.

To conclude about Eigil Knuth's motivation: His first and foremost motivation for surveying the Thule region was to find the first Palaeo-Eskimo migration route into West Greenland. Secondly, it was to record a type of shelter ruin, belonging to an, as yet unknown but presumed, third Palaeo-Eskimo migration.

1.1.3 Previous work from the Thule region that inspired Eigil Knuth

Holtved states that the Dorset culture was the first migration into the Thule region (Holtved 1944: part II: 39). Holtved could document the existence of the Dorset culture in the Thule region, due to discoveries of Dorset artefacts below and mixed into Thule houses and Thule middens, which he excavated in Inglefield Land. However, Holtved never became aware of true Dorset houses.

Captain George Comer, who from 1913–18 found and excavated house ruins and middens from Parker Snow Bay (76° 10′ N) to Rensselaer Harbour in Inglefield Land (78° 40′ N), also came across artefacts that particularly interested Eigil Knuth (Holtved 1944 and 1954). In Rensselaer Bay, Comer found a cloven foot lance with an inserted side blade; an artefact Knuth knew was typical for Independence II and Dorset I (Greenlandic Dorset). Moreover, among the finds at Etah, Comer found a convex scraper and a spalled burin without grinding. Artefacts that Eigil Knuth knew were certain proof of an early Palaeo-Eskimo occupation.

From these previous investigations Knuth was able to deduct:

Just like Holtved's Dorset examples, the Comer flint finds came from Neo-Eskimo ruin sites, and the comparison of the two archaeologists' material indicated that Palaeo-Eskimos <u>must</u> have passed through the Thule district in two different periods. A more definite clarification would require the finding of their settlement sites. (Eigil Knuth's manuscript 1977)

To conclude, Eigil Knuth had indications from artefacts in the Thule region which he could relate to two early Palaeo-Eskimo migrations into Greenland. And he concluded that the evidence pointed to migration, based on the argument that Palaeo-Eskimos (Saqqaq and Dorset I) *must* have passed through the Thule region to arrive in Disko Bugt.

1.1.4 Eigil Knuth's introduction to the archaeology at Nuulliit

Eigil Knuth resumed his field trips in the Thule region and his final discovery and investigation of the Palaeo-Eskimo sites at Nuulliit was as follows:

> With this aim in mind, when the journeys to and from Peary Land in the summers of 1952–58 required a stopover on Thule Air Base, the author carried out expeditions in and around the Thule district. During these fieldwork opportunities, attention was given to raised, 'sub-fossil' strand terraces at 6–20 metres height above the current beach level, and it emerged in many areas that at this height level, tent rings were situated, and a thick growth of lichens on the stones indicated a considerable age. At the same time these dark large-lobed lichens, in conditions favourable for fertile growth, are precisely the reason that the evidence for the Palaeo-Eskimo origin of the tent rings, in the form of flint tools or flint chips, were not to be found.
>
> This was the case for the tent rings discovered on the Umanaqhalvø, the tent rings on the south coast of Wolstenholme Fjord, near Narssârssuk 12 km southwest of Thule Air Base, in Parker Snow Bay 42 km south of the base, and the tent sites in Booth Sound, that are cut into the outer coast of Steensby Land, approximately mid-way between Wolstenholme Fjord and Inglefield Gulf (figure 1.2).
>
> The attempts to find dwelling remains of indisputable Palaeo-Eskimo character finally bore fruit in 1958 at Nûgdlit where Holtved, 11 years earlier, excavated a Neo-Eskimo settlement site of 62 house ruins, that he considered to be 'the largest hitherto known ruin site in Greenland'. The Palaeo-Eskimo structures at the site were in association with a gravel terrace and a number of gravel terraces just a couple of metres from Holtved's ruins, and

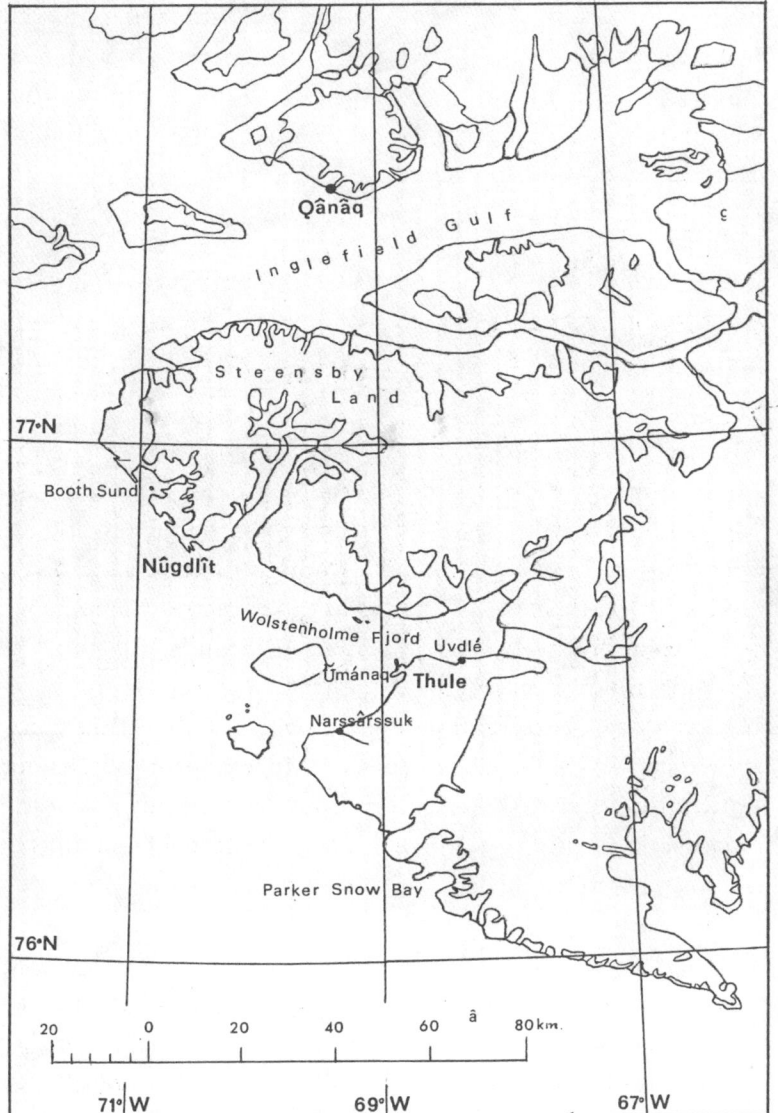

1.2
The Thule region. Drawing E. Knuth

his stone rings, which unfortunately only contained very few flint tools, were divided into 'group I' (Plateau A, C, D, E, F) and 'group II' (Plateau H, B and area I) in two levels, that correspond to two cultures and two cultural epochs (figures 1.3 & 2.0).

Considering the differences between the site and the grassy lower lying neo-Eskimo ruin terrain, in terms of the quaternary geology and the archaeology, it would be natural to name the Palaeo-Eski-

THE FIELD OF RESEARCH

1.3
Photo of the Nuulliit peninsula. Photo E. Knuth

mo domain as 'Old Nûgdlît'. It was estimated, in 1958, to consist of 36 stone rings, but after two later visits to the place, in 1960 and 1975, the number has grown to 49, divided between 30 of the earlier culture (group I) and 14 of the later (group II).

If we join these two non-contemporary groups together with their direct continuation in New Nûgdlît's three ruin groups, outermost on 'West Point', the little Nûgdlît peninsula can then not just be called, until now, the largest known Greenlandic ruin site, but becomes the place in Greenland that, until now, has the longest proven continuity, reaching far back in time, in its settlement history.
(Introduction to Eigil Knuth's 1977 manuscript)

1.1.5 Eigil Knuth's four seasons at Nuulliit

1958

After surveying the southern parts of the Thule region from 1952, and especially the area around Dundas and Wolstenholme Fjord, Eigil Knuth was eager to continue his search for Palaeo-Eskimo evidence along the coasts of Steensby Land. In 1958, he was on his way with the American sea-ice breaker 'Atka' from Hall Land where he had been excavating the Solbakken site. He was heading towards Uummannaq, Thule Airbase, to catch a flight back to Copenhagen. However, he somehow persuaded the captain to lift him off onto Booth Sound, at Steensby Land, with a helicopter. At Booth Sound two houses, built from local wood of bad quality, were inhabited by Eskimo families. Knuth stayed for some days, surveying in the Booth Sound including Hoppner Ness, and he found several structures which were old, but he always ended his descriptions with a disappointed: 'no flint was found'. After some days he made an appointment with the local Inughuit to ship him down to Nuulliit. He was inspired by Holtved's statement that lack of time made it impossible for Holtved to excavate what he perceived were the oldest ruins at Nuulliit, but in his diary he also mentions that Meldgaard has recommended him to survey this site. The Inughuit Jess, his oldest boy Pilutaq and the Inughuit Maissanguaq shipped him down to Nuulliit on 21 August (figure 1.4).

1.4
Knuth's tent in Both Sund 1958.
Photo E. Knuth

During the excavation of ruin nos. 48 and 49 in Holtved's group III, Eigil Knuth often had to wait for the perma-frozen floor layers to melt. In the meantime he surveyed the beach terraces on the Nuulliit peninsula. In his diary he writes that on some of the terraces there is a 'smell of the Palaeo-Eskimos', and he is, whenever the sun is low, using his sun reflection method to survey for flint. On 25 August he found a lithic harpoon end blade with a concave base at the H-plateau. Soon he left the ruins in Group III and started excavating structures at the H-plateau, but only to be disappointed: 'no flint was found'. One evening, on his way back from the H-plateau, he crossed a higher plateau and discovered a stemmed end blade made from grey-white microcrystalline quarts (mcq). At this plateau he also discovered several tent rings. Eigil Knuth never got the chance to investigate the ruins at the F-plateau more thoroughly in 1958, although he found a few more flakes. Already on 26 August, Knuth had made an appointment with a man, Ingmar, from Qaanaaq who was sailing from Qaanaaq to Thule Airbase, to pick him up on his way, at Nuulliit. However, when a boat arrived 'Ingmar' was not on the boat himself. Six Inughuit, four males and two females, on their way to Thule Airbase, were asked to pick up Knuth, and he thus joined the party down to Thule Airbase. On the way he took a few spectacular photos of the crew (figures 1.5, 1.6).

1.5
Knuth's tent at Nuulliit 1958.
Photo E. Knuth

1.6 Returning to the Thule base by boat with local Inuit: *Maigssánguaq, Petaq, Ussarqak* and the girl Simigaq. Photo taken by E. Knuth at 3 a.m. on 27 August 1958

1960

In 1960, Eigil Knuth took advantage of the new possibilities for logistics at the Thule Airbase and was landed at Nuulliit by an impressive Piasecki helicopter (figure 1.7). He landed on 27 August and was picked up by the helicopter five days later (2/8). During this season, Knuth was determined to excavate the Palaeo-Eskimo tent rings at the F-plateau that he had discovered shortly before he left in 1958. He started excavating ruins at the F-plateau: F4, F6 and F7. He discovered and surface collected ruins at the D-plateau, D1 and D2, and discovered the I-area. Knuth's most precious single find this season was a narrow lithic arrowhead found in ruin F7. The morphology of this artefact made Knuth, for the first time, wonder about Denbigh Culture in the Thule area. Knuth had good summer weather at Nuulliit in 1960, and his diary reveals many ideas, thoughts and inspirations for future projects. Finally, he was picked up again by the pilot, W.A. Britton, and flown back to Thule Airbase (figure 1.8).

1975

During the 1975 season, Eigil Knuth turned 72, but he was still very active. During this season he planned to go to Washington Land, sharing logistics with geologists from the Geological Survey of Greenland. He invited a friend, Erik Hoff, to join and help him during this field campaign. Erik Hoff was a lawyer but also a dedicat-

1.7
Arriving at Nuulliit from the Thule airbase in 1960. A Piasecki helicopter called the 'Banana' transported Knuth. Photo E. Knuth

ed sportsman who had joined and planned several sports expeditions to Greenland, some of these with participation of Knuth. Erik Hoff was 69 years old during the summer of 1975. An interesting perspective on the 1975 campaign is that Hoff kept a diary during the stay at Nuulliit, which he later partly published together with his memories from his sports expeditions (Hoff 1992). Thus we have, we might say, a second opinion on the stay at Nuulliit in 1975.

The weather conditions at the Thule Airbase made it impossible to go to Washington Land, and the plans were changed so that they instead headed for the close lying Nuulliit peninsula. Knuth was not particularly sorry for this change, as he considered the entire Greenland as his field of investigation (Erik Hoff's comment); however, Hoff was disappointed. Knuth and Hoff were transported with a 'Bell helicopter' and stayed at Nuulliit from 12 July until 28 August, in total 47 days. Thus the 1975 season must be considered as the main season at Nuulliit. During this season Knuth discovered ruins at six more plateaus and renamed the ruin groups from A-I. He excavated nos. A1, A2, C2 (partly), C3, D1 (partly), E2, F3 (partly), F4 (partly), and surface collected ruin nos. C1, F1, F2. Hoff assisted Knuth with the measuring of ruin positions and surveying, but carried out no excavations, as he was not interested in archaeology. Generally the weather conditions

1.8
Knuth's tent at Nuulliit in 1960. Photo E. Knuth

were very bad during the 1975 season at Nuulliit. It was cold, often freezing, the wind was generally very strong and Nuulliit was hit by several storms, the last one being a snowstorm. Hoff and Knuth were proud men, each of them sleeping in their own tent, and they did not complain or ask each other for help, even though Hoff's tent at one stage broke completely. Generally they both were considerably affected by the cold, especially during the nights, and their equipment was not at all appropriate for the conditions. Hoff made one-day expeditions, whenever the weather allowed, while Knuth excavated. Knuth considered the archaeological results as meagre, probably because he had to work hard to find artefacts and understand the structure of the ruins, in contrast to Peary Land. However, he also made some extraordinary and interesting single finds, e.g. a large adze preform made from dolerite.

Generally Erik Hoff's diary leaves an impression of a tough and troublesome season and Eigil Knuth being in a troublesome mood. However, there are also a few glimpses of pleasant moments at Nuulliit in Hoff's diary, e.g when Knuth and Hoff are having a glass of whisky while listening to Bellman's songs from a small tape recorder in Knuth's tent (figure 1.9).

THE FIELD OF RESEARCH

1.9
Knuth and Erik Hoff's tents at Nuulliit after a snowstorm in 1975. Photo E. Knuth

1990

In 1990 Eigil Knuth returned to Nuulliit, at the age of 87. His conclusions, especially concerning the radiocarbon dating, had been questioned and he could not allow any doubts about his work and consequently had to return. During this campaign he invited two students in prehistoric archaeology, Tim Grønnegaard and Claus Kjeld Jensen, to help him with excavations and drawings of the ruins. Especially due to the work of the two students, the 1990 season was very productive in many ways. However, Knuth's primary goal, to bring samples of prehistoric organic materials for radiocarbon dating was not met.

During this season, ruin nos. A2 and C2 were re-excavated, while C1, D2, F9, B2, B6, B7, B8 were excavated. Thule Eskimo skeletal material was discovered. Moreover, several plans and drawings of ruins were finished and much photo registration was done. From ruin C1, a small sample of charcoal was taken. In connection with this project, the sample has been AMS dated (KIA 32917) (figure 1.10).

THE FIELD OF RESEARCH

1.10 The tent camp at Nuulliit in 1990. Photo E. Knuth

1.1.6 How artefacts and documentation from Nuulliit were re-investigated and a new interpretation of the prehistory at Nuulliit emerged

The source material

As mentioned earlier, Knuth left substantial material from his investigations at Nuulliit:

    An artefact collection mostly consisting of lithic artefacts

    Photographs of structures at Nuulliit

    Drawings and plans of excavated structures

    Radiocarbon dates

    Diaries from the field campaigns

    An unpublished and incomplete manuscript

My task was to re-analyse the archaeological material from Nuulliit, that Eigil Knuth collected, and to view this material from a modern scientific perspective. However, parts of Knuth's manuscript were complete, and he was a splendid author. His descriptions of field trips, the landscape, the excavation procedures and interpretations were relevant to this text. Thus substantial parts of Knuth's own text is untouched in this volume, in particular chapters including descriptions and first hand observations.

During re-examination, all material from Nuulliit was classified and registered, as if for the first time. Eigil Knuth had focused on single artefacts and described these with text and photos. 'Spectacular artefacts' from different contexts, different ruins and plateaus were thus depicted on plates and photographs by Knuth as a kind of representative collection of the site. This kind of documentation is a problem today when we are interested in the context of the find as the starting point for investigation and interpretation. Therefore, a series of new photos of all artefacts from each single context (ruin) was produced. Twenty new, high quality photographs, presented in chapter 2.0, completed this documentation.

The architecture of the ruins was an important topic in Eigil Knuth's research, and his documentation of this subject is generally of a high quality. However, on this matter we have to rely completely on Knuth's information since the ruins were severely disturbed during excavation. In this volume, Knuth's data concerning architecture, including ground plans of ruins from Nuulliit, are published. The architecture will not be elaborated on in this volume, but hopefully future work will be carried out concerning the cultural aspects reflected in the variations of structures at Old Nuulliit. The lithic material was chosen as the primary source for an investigation of the cultural history at Nuulliit, as explained below.

The *chaîne opératoire* approach
During the last decade a new methodology, the dynamical technological analysis, also called the *'chaînes opératoires* approach', has been introduced for the study of lithic technology in Stone Age societies (Pelegrin et al. 1988; Pelegrin 1990; Inizian et al. 1999). This methodology focuses on the prehistoric knowledge embedded in the production of the lithic material and the specific technological choices taken during the production process. Thus, by perceiving and investigating lithic artefacts as processes, different social traditions, which share and transmit (technological) knowledge can be described (Madsen 1992; Pelegrin 1995; Sørensen 2006b; Sørensen 2006; Sørensen 2011). The *chaînes opératoires* approach is especially fruitful when applied to crafts from Arctic prehistory, due to an astonishing accuracy and specific manufacturing process in the Palaeo-Eskimo tradition (Sørensen 2006b). Moreover, results derived from using this methodology have already resulted in the recognition of two new Palaeo-Eskimo traditions in Greenland (Pre-Dorset and Canadian Early Dorset in the Thule area) and have questioned former interpretations of differences between typologically defined cultures such as Independence II and Dorset I (Grønnow and Sørensen 2006; Sørensen 2006a; Sørensen 2011).

The lithic artefact material from Nuulliit was studied and classified using a dynamical technological methodology approach. Terminology and methodology for this classification, in relation to the Palaeo-Eskimo cultures, is described thoroughly in Sørensen 2006a and Sørensen 2011.

Absolute dating
The radiocarbon dating that was made from Nuulliit on Eigil Knuth's initiative was highly problematic, mainly due to the selected material. Formerly, large samples of organic material were needed for conventional radiocarbon dating, while the modern AMS radiocarbon method only needs very small samples to produce precise results. Previously, marine samples and charcoal from driftwood were dated, but today we carefully select the materials, so that only bone from terrestrial species and local grown twigs with a low own age are sampled, in order to produce reliable absolute datings.

A few new dates of material from Old Nuulliit have been made since Knuth visited Nuulliit. Two were made by Schledermann and McCullough (1992) from a hearth row and from ruin F7, and another one in relation to this project: charcoal of local willow, from ruin C1, collected by Knuth and his assistants in 1990. The dating, and especially the discussion of which dates are to be trusted, plays an important role in the interpretation of the cultural history of Nuulliit, especially since Knuth's own arguments were based on the dating. Absolute dating will be reported and discussed in chapter 2.3.

So, this volume is a re-examination of the Nuulliit material based on artefacts and documentation provided by Eigil Knuth during four field seasons. His original documentation is, for the most part, published. The analytical principle favoured is that every ruin including artefacts and information is described both separately and in relation to other ruins and ruin groups at Old Nuulliit. On this basis interpretations are made. The documentation of the site is detailed and new alternative interpretations hopefully develop from this publication.

Studies of the lithic artefact material using a *chaîne opératoire* approach form the analytical basis. This methodology provides the opportunity to relate lithic inventories to prehistoric craft traditions. The methodology has recently provided substantial new results in relation to Greenland's prehistory and it opens up for more detailed social and cultural studies. Radiocarbon dating from Nuulliit is critically reviewed and a new AMS dating is made to elucidate the absolute chronology of Old Nuulliit.

1.2 The Environment at Nuulliit

1.2.1 Environmental preconditions for a hunter-gatherer society at Nuulliit: the sea-ice situation

For a prehistoric population subsisting almost exclusively on food resources obtained through hunting, a close association between the location of settlements and proximity to game was important. In the High Arctic, where the primary game has been marine mammals, sea-ice conditions are thus extremely important for the precise location and abundance of the game and thereby for the prehistoric settlements.

The ice conditions in the Smith Sund region are determined by the interplay between factors such as: sea currents, wind, tide, icebergs, sea depth, salinity, climate, and solar radiation. Thus even though the climate is an important factor for the formation of open water areas, other factors determine *where* the ice will break first, and where the ice will have a tendency to be unstable or absent even during the coldest periods of the year.

Many types of open water areas exist from Baffin Bugt to Smith Sund: A non-linear opening, enclosed in ice, is called a 'polynya', yet if it occurs in the same position every year it is called a 'recurring polynya'. If a polynya is limited to one side by the coast it is called a 'shore polynya', but if it is limited by fast ice in the open area it is called a 'flaw polynya'. Moreover, polynyas that are open only few weeks before a general ice break are defined as 'secondary polynyas' (Schledermann 1980).

The information about where and when polynyas appeared was part of traditional Inuit knowledge. This knowledge has been recorded and sometimes also experienced, in the 20th century by biologists and ethnologists (Vibe 1950; Schledermann 1980; Gilberg 1994). A modern tool for monitoring ice conditions is by satellite photos (http://rapidfire.sci.gsfc.nasa.gov/gallery/?search=greenland). However, probably due to lack of daylight, satellite photos from the High Arctic are only provided from April to September.

The following analysis of the ice conditions outside Steensby Land and Nuulliit is primarily based upon recordings of the ice from 1939–41 by C. Vibe (1950), together with studies of satellite photos of the sea between north Greenland and northeast Canada, from April to September 2001–2004.

In Smith Sund and Baffin Bugt a great recurrent polynya, called the North Water, appears early in spring. Satellite photos show that the ice begins to recede in the most northern part of Smith Sund, and in Kane Basin, during April. At the same time the ice is breaking up from Cape Alexander and down to Melville Bay, leaving an open water zone between fast ice and the massive drift ice in the North Water polynia. True shore polynyas are formed along the coasts of Ellesmere Island and in the fjords, e.g. Flagler Bay and Camperdown polynya (Schledermann 1980). The open water zone in the North Water is generally situated many kilometres from land; however, on the Greenland side, off Inglefield Land, Northumberland Ø and Steensby Land, the open water zone is formed quite close to land. In the middle of April, the North Water polynya opens (see figure 1.11) and by the end of May it has extended considerably. From Steensby Land down to Nuulliit, Smith Sund is ice-

1.11
The sea ice and the forming of polynias between north Greenland and Canada, 11 April 2002

THE FIELD OF RESEARCH

1.12
The sea ice and the forming of polynias between north Greenland and Canada, 25 May 2001

free (figure 1.12). However, ice is still lying solid in the fjords, i.e. Granville Fjord and Wolstenholme Fjord. From July to the beginning of August the fjords finally break up (figure 1.13).

During winter the North Water is generally covered with drift ice and frozen sea ice, but due to several factors, e.g. sea currents and tides, polynyas are, now and then, formed in Smith Sund, especially during the new and full moon. According to Vibe's recordings from 1939–41, polynyas that are open during winter appear in the North Water, between Agpârssuit and Northumberland Ø and others are open for almost the whole winter, between Northumberland Ø and Herbert Ø. Close to Washington Land, near Cape Calhoun and between Ellesmere Island and Kent Island, polynyas are present during winter (Vibe 1950).

Observations and satellite photos show that no local recurrent polynyas are formed off Nuulliit. Thus it is not possible to explain the large settlements at Nuul-

1.13
The sea ice and the forming of polynias between north Greenland and Canada, 31 July 2002

liit by a recurrent polynya formed during early spring as on e.g. Ellesmere Island or in Northeast Greenland (Schledermann 1980; Schledermann 1990; Sørensen and Andreasen 2006). What then is the reason for the substantial habitation by both Palaeo-Eskimo traditions and the Thule Culture at this location? One answer is that Nuulliit is situated in an outer fjord, which is closer to the ice edge of the large North Water polynya, than many other sites in the Thule region. Thus, it might have been possible to carry out ice edge hunting, either during one-day trips, or during a several day tour from Nuulliit, depending on the season and the ice conditions. However Vibe also provides a description of an additional open water mechanism, which, during winters, possibly has affected the sea in front of the Nuulliit site considerably (Vibe 1950: 15). The sea depth outside the flat Nuulliit peninsula is rather low, 40–80 m. This means that the larger icebergs will gather on banks, grounded often for several years, off Nuulliit. The grounded icebergs contribute to a rapid scattering of the ice in the spring, since the tide will keep the water open around them. Often icebergs will float about, moving with the current, whereby they churn up the ice around them. From personal experience and recording Vibe writes: 'In the winter the tidal cracks round the stranded icebergs are filled with seals, often also walruses, which here always have natural breathing holes' (Vibe 1950: 16). The large winter settlements from the Thule Culture, and maybe also the Palaeo-Eskimo settlements, at Nuulliit, can therefore be explained by the presence of open water and cracks in the ice, due to tidal sea movements in combination with grounded icebergs outside the Nuulliit peninsula, providing extraordinary living conditions for the marine mammals. Especially the walruses are favoured by these conditions, but also polar bears that live from sea mammals gain from this situation.

1.2.2 The climate in the prehistoric period

From reconstructed temperature curves based on ice core data (Dahl-Jensen et al. 1998), it can be seen that the first Palaeo-Eskimos arrived in Greenland during the last part of the Holocene climatic optimum, lasting from 6000–2000 BC. This period was seemingly stable and about 2.5°C warmer than today. From the end of the climatic optimum and until year 1 BC, the temperatures steadily cooled to around 0.5°C below present temperatures. This lowering was followed by a warming with a maximum around AD 1000 (the medieval warming), around 1°C warmer than today and dropping again by 0.5° and 0.7° into the 'Little Ice Age', ending during the mid 19th century (figure 1.14).

However, the ice core data also indicate that the High Arctic climate generally seems to have been more stable than in Arctic and sub Arctic Greenland (Dahl-Jensen et al. 1998).

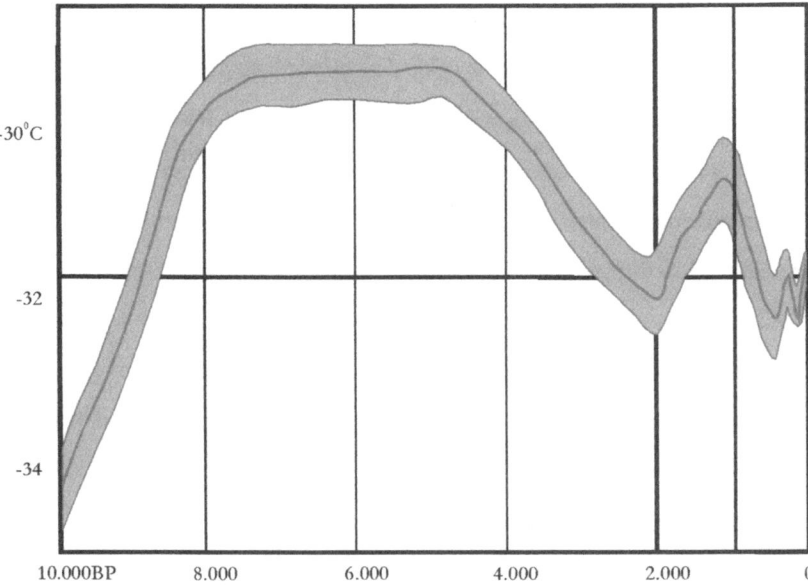

1.14 The Holocene climate curve measured directly at the Greenland inland ice (GRIP). Adapted by M. Appelt from Dahl-Jensen et al. 1998

1.2.3 Marine and terrestrial resources in the Nuulliit area

The walrus (*Odobenus rosmarus*) has from historic time been recorded as stationary in the Thule region, and faunal analyses of prehistoric material show that the walrus already thrived in the region when the first Palaeo-Eskimo population migrated into the area, 2500 BC (e.g. at Solbakken site) (Grønnow and Jensen 2003). The distribution and migration of the walrus population within the area was thoroughly investigated by Vibe (1950) and Born (2005), who also describe changes in the distribution related to either intensified hunting using firearms or changes in nutrition. According to Vibe (1950: 23ff.) walrus migrate between the Melville Bugt and Smith Sund. During early summer walruses feed, while migrating northwards from the Melville Bugt. Due to the ice conditions this happens far from land. However, when the walruses reach Wolstenholme Ø and Saunders Ø in June, the ice has receded and they stay here for a longer period. From July to September they again become rare in this area, leaving for Smith Sund, gathering outside Northumberland Ø, Inglefield Land up to Washington Land and Ellesmere Island. In the middle of September the walruses return to Saunders Ø. The walruses forage at depths down to 80 m. In the Thule region the sea bottom down to 80 m often consists of old landmass covered with moraine material, that has lowered, and this forms a favourable substratum for a rich fauna, and thereby rich nutrition for the walrus population. One of the largest walrus areas in the Thule region is located between Wolstenholme Fjord and Kap Parry at Steensby Land. The depths do not exceed 60 m here and the bottom sediments are mixed with moraine material rich in nutrition. There are only a few places the walruses come up on land, one being Littleton Ø in Smith Sund. Another place is at Uvdle in Wolstenholme Fjord, about 50 km from Nuulliit.

During the winter, the walruses remain as close to the banks as possible. As soon as the ice becomes more than 10–15 cm thick, the walruses have to retire to greater depths. As the winter becomes colder the walruses come into the coast when the ice occasionally breaks, but in February they generally must retire to the ice edges. The only places where the walruses can winter are at the Neqe banks, the Etah banks and in an area west of Wolstenholme Ø.

It must be emphasised that the distribution and migration of the walrus could have changed through time in the Thule area. However, the prime factor determining the abundance and distribution of the walrus is the nutritious moraine banks between 40–80 m, which are typical of the Thule region. These banks must have existed through the entire Holocene period. It therefore seems likely that walruses have been potential game at the coasts outside Steensby Land, when the first people entered the region. If the same migration pattern existed in prehistoric times as recorded in modern times, the walrus could have been hunted off Nuulliit particularly in June and again in September. However, depending on the prehistoric ice conditions, walruses probably stayed during the winter outside Wolstenholme Ø, and could therefore well have been hunted in openings in the ice off Nuulliit during the year.

Bearded seal (*Erignathus barbatus*)
The bearded seal is stationary in the Thule region. The bearded seal lived off Nuulliit both during winters and summers in the 20th century, being numerous here compared to other places in the Thule region. This seal is omnivorous and the sea-bottom fauna plays an important role in its diet. The bearded seal never goes on land and only seldom on ice, thus it must be caught at its breathing hole or in open water. The bearded seal favours open water situations although it can live far from the ice edges during winter as long as cracks are constantly appearing in the ice. The breathing holes seldom appear in ice thicker than 20–30 cm.

The harp seal (*Phoca groenlandica*)
The harp seal is a summer guest in the Thule region, living from polar cod in the fjords. No information concerning this seal can be related to the Nuulliit area.

The ringed seal (*Phoca hispida*)
This seal is extremely common in the Thule region, and historically much human subsistence was based on this prey. The ringed seal is stationary in the region and has a somewhat even distribution. It is not bound to particular sea depths or ice conditions and is able to maintain breathing holes through 2 m thick ice. No specific information concerning this seal can be related to the Nuulliit area.

Narwhal (*Monodon monoceros*)
The narwhal arrives in the Thule region during spring migration along the coast of both Thule and Ellesmere Island. During summer the narwhal lives in the fjords, especially in Inglefield Bredning, where it breeds, and feeds from halibut. At Nuulliit it is possible to hunt migrating narwhals in spring, i.e. in May. This could also have been the case formerly.

Caribou (*Rangifer tarandus groenlandicus*)
Knud Rasmussen (1921) mentions that caribou have been especially numerous north of the Pituffik Glacier, Saunders Ø, south of Wolstenholme Fjord, around Olrik Fjord and in Inglefield Land. However, caribou are subject to marked population fluctuations. Whether caribou ever had a substantial population on Steensby Land cannot be determined, but historically areas close to Nuulliit, such as Saun-

ders Ø, and land south of Wolstenholme Fjord, have been well known as caribou hunting grounds.

Musk ox (*Ovibos moschatus*)
Musk oxen entered Greenland around 3000 BC, and were formerly distributed in the entire Thule region, including Steensby Land, and along the north east coast of Greenland down to Scoresby Sund (Bennike and Andreasen 2005). During Eigil Knuth's surveys in the Thule area, he came across skeletal remains of several musk oxen, which document this information. Exactly when musk oxen lived in Steensby Land and when they became extinct in the southern Thule region cannot be determined.

Polar bear (*Ursus maritimus*)
Polar bears have traditionally been valued game in the Thule region (Gilberg 1994). There are two areas in the Thule region where polar bears are especially numerous and have been successfully hunted: The north side of the Humboldt Gletcher and between Parker Snow Bay and the Melville Bay in the southern Thule region (Appelt et al. 2001). The southern area starts about 100 km south of Nuulliit. Often the polar bear is hunted in September and October when it comes close to the coasts to catch seals in the open water between the sea ice and productive glaciers. Some of the earliest polar bear bones in the Thule region are from Solbakken site in Hall Land, related to the Independence I culture, approximately 2000 BC (Grønnow and Jensen 2003). Thus it can be expected that polar bears have been in the Thule and the Nuulliit area in prehistoric times.

Birds
The Thule region is dominated by little auk (*Alle alle*). Today it is estimated that, from Parker Snow bay to Etah, this area hosts around 30 million pairs of little auk during the summer (Salomonsen 1981). The little auk lives in colonies at large cliffs near the open sea. Traditionally the little auk has been an important and stable food reserve in the Thule region. Older people, especially, could live near the little auk colonies during the summer and thereby have easy access to food. Generally the mouths of the fjords are inhabited by large amounts of waterfowl such as birds from the auk family (guillemot, puffin) and from the gull family, while eider ducks live on small islands near the coast. At present it has not been possible to document colonies of birds near Nuulliit, but the mouth of Wolstenholme Fjord is an obvious biotope for breeding sea birds.

THE FIELD OF RESEARCH

1.2.4 Geography and landscape

Steensby Land, on which Nuulliit forms the most south-westerly point, is a peninsula shooting out into the northern Baffin Bugt, limited by Inglefield Gulf to the north and Wolstenholme Fjord to the south (figure 1.15). The Steensby peninsula is about 100 km long from east to west and 40 km across. Steensby Land is partly covered by the Inland Ice all the way down to Nuulliit. In fact it is possible to enter the Inland Ice from Nuulliit during winter and spring, when the sea ice is broken, a situation Holtved took advantage of when leaving from his first visits at Nuulliit (Holtved 1954).

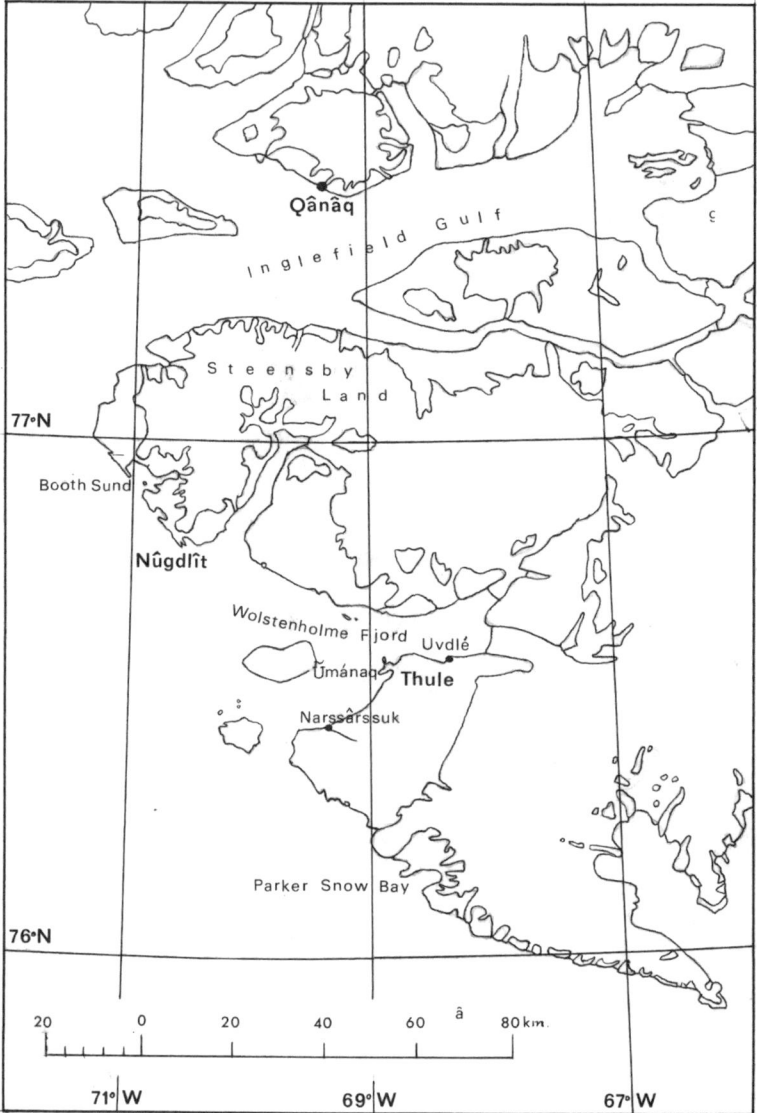

1.15
The Thule area in which Eigil surveyed from 1952–58. Drawing E. Knuth

Nuulliit
The Nûgdlît peninsula
(76° 48' 7.5" N., 70° 35' 15" W.)
'Nuulliit' is Greenlandic and means 'those who live at the land's end' and is a specific term for the outermost spit of land where the Thule winter houses are located (New Nuulliit). However, today the whole foreland bears the name Nuulliit. Eigil Knuth describes the location of Nuulliit as follows:

The Inland Ice at Steensby Land extends, west of Granville Fjord, in an enormous glacial tongue down towards the country's southwestern corner, where the Nûgdlît peninsula is situated. This low peninsula terminates outermost in two parallel-running points, W (West Point) and E (East Point), whose east sides are marked by moraine ridges, lying on a foundation of intrusive dolerite columns. Apart from these two ridges, the surface takes the form of a network of low plateaus, some sandy, some stony, that arc and bend around each other, resulting in numerous lakes of a variety of sizes. (Knuth 1977) (figure 1.3)

1.2.5 Geology and geological resources

Steensby Land, where Nuulliit is located at its southern shore, is part of a geological formation called the 'Thule Super group' consisting mainly of shale, sandstone, siltstone and dolerites but occasionally also, in the north-western part of Steensby Land, volcanic rock. Within the area several dykes and sills of the basalt-like material 'dolerite' is present.

The local geology at Nuulliit consists of dolerite bedrock and marine deposits from raised beach terraces. Due to isostatic uplifts of the low-lying foreland at Nuulliit, the area is covered with beach-rolled boulders mainly of dolerite.

The type of geology at Steensby Land, consisting of silt, shale and sandstone sometimes in combination with basaltic formations, is a potentially rich area for lithic materials used by Palaeo-Eskimos for tool production, i.e. stones with conchoidal fracture. Even though the lithic technology changed towards the grinding of schists and siltstones in the Thule Culture and finally disappeared with the emergence of European iron, there are still place names used in the Nuulliit area which indicate the former importance of these geological resources. The original Inuit term for a stone which splits with conchoidal fracture and is used for tools is 'Angmâq', and at the west coast of Steensby Land close to Hoppner Ness a locality is traditionally called 'Angmârsiorfik', indicating that at this place 'Angmâq' can be found (Holtved 1954). Considering the local geology near Hoppner Ness, this source of lithic material is a compressed (metamorphous) schist, today often termed 'killiaq'. Geological descriptions of the area mention the appearance of agate, i.e. microcrystalline quarts with a conchoidal fracture, in Barden Bugt at the northeast corner of Steensby Land. Furthermore, the geological map suggests the appearance of microcrystalline quartz (chert) at two localities on the northern shore of Steensby Land (Dawes 2006). Whether these sources have the appropriate quality and size for prehistoric tool manufacture is yet unknown. However, their appearance suggests that the geology within the region had some importance for the Palaeo-Eskimo population.

Another important material, which was traditionally collected by the Polar-Eskimo, between Granville Fjord and Booth Sund, was pyrite (Holtved 1954). Pyrite was used by the Palaeo-Eskimo traditions and during the Thule Culture to strike for fire (Stapert and Johansen 1999).

1.3 Eigil Knuth's first surveys to find Palaeo-Eskimos in the Thule region, 1952–1958

Eigil Knuth's surveys in the Thule region, before he discovered Old Nuulliit, is well described by Knuth himself in his 1977 manuscript. His experiences in this period have an interesting historical dimension because he reports from the Thule region precisely in the same period as the local Inughuit population at Uummannaq was being deported to Qaanaaq, and as the Thule Airbase was built up, resulting in significant cultural and natural changes in the region.

Before the presentation of Nûgdlît's Palaeo-Eskimo ruin groups, a number of the insights that were made during expeditions from the Thule Airbase, partly during work in the field, and partly during dialogue with the Eskimos, should be described:

The Umanak peninsula, 1952–53 (figures 1.15 & 1.16)
The first stay in Thule coincided with the events concerning the incorporation of the Umanak peninsula in the airbase's defence system and the moving of the Umanak settlement's Eskimos over 100 km north to Qarnak in Inglefield Bay. The journey to the Peary Land region in the month of May 1952 took place before this move, as the terrain on the peninsula lay still undisturbed, and the local life between the Polar Eskimos and the Danes still

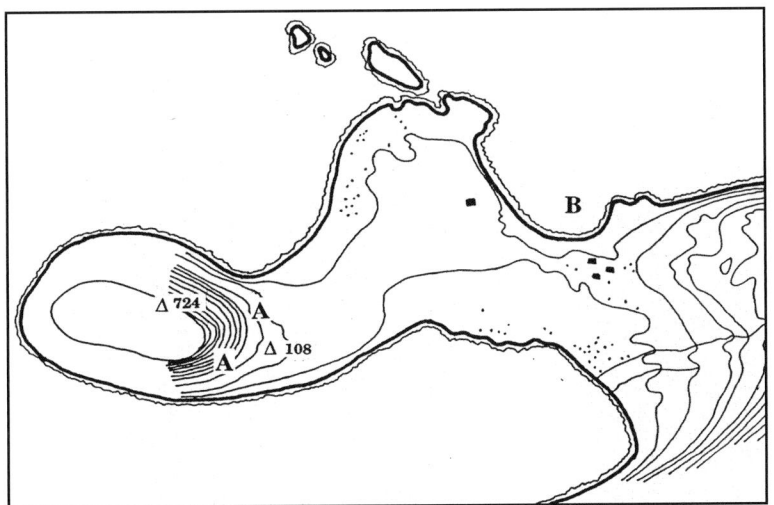

1.16
The Dundas peninsula at Uummannaq in 1952. Drawing E. Knuth

took place within the framework that Knud Rasmussen had created with his trading and mission station 'Thule'.

On the way home from Peary Land some months later in 1952, we had the opportunity to visit a couple of the veterans from the great expeditions in their homes: the 64-year-old Odak, who was with Peary at the North Pole in 1909, and Inukitsupaluk and Qâvigarssuak, who accompanied Knud Rasmussen, on the 2nd and the 5th Thule expeditions respectively. I showed Odak and the 51-year-old Qissuk some of the 4000-year-old flint objects from the time of Independence I, found in Peary Land, but neither of the two men had seen similar objects in the Thule district. This seems remarkable, bearing in mind the Eskimos' sharp eyes, and when we remember that the Greenlanders in Disko Bugt and in the Upernavik district, over many generations, had collected flint objects and delivered them to the Danish officials.

In Qâvigarssuak's house the older folk could, on the other hand, relate that within their lifetime, there has been a lowering of the land and a considerable retreat of the glaciers.

The short visits to the peninsula in 1952 allowed only a superficial going over of the raised strand terraces, where traces of Palaeo-Eskimo settlements might be found. Tent rings that appeared to be of considerable age were observed at several places, where the terraces were beautifully preserved, for example in a small bay ('B' in fig. 1.16) north of the radio station, and at the foot of the Umanak mountain, that once had been an island. The search for flint objects was without result, and the possibility for identifying their presence was made difficult by the previously mentioned dense growth of large lobed, grey lichen that covered the stony ground everywhere.

The following year, 1953, the Eskimo settlements lay abandoned, and the whole surface of the peninsula was scraped and ploughed by bulldozers, so nothing of its original structure remained.

Wolstenholme Fjord's south coast, 1958
On the first promontory east of the Umanak peninsula, 6–7 metres

1.17
Tent house from the south shore of Wolstenholme fjord 1958. Photo E. Knuth

over sea level, were two rectangular hunter's shelters of the Shelter type, built of dense stone walling. With internal dimensions of c. 150 × 200 cm they were covered by a layer of moss. Flint objects were not found (figure 1.17).

At the valley to the west, that serves, in winter, as a sled route up to the Inland Ice for travellers to Kap York, on a system of undisturbed strand terraces, a number of very sunken tent rings were seen. One of these, at a height of 8 metres above sea level, had white quartz stones in the middle of the flooring. Flint objects were not found.

On the route from here, along the strand towards Uvdle also at a height of 8 meters, a tent ring was situated, that was completely overgrown with black, large-lobed lichen. A scraping of this growth allowed that a floor of quite large flagstones appeared, but there were no flint object to be seen.

By Uvdle (figure 1.15) (where Holtved has excavated a house ruin) lay what is apparently the oldest tent ring c. 6 metres above sea level, totally overgrown with dark lichens. It had a rectangular outline measuring 150 × 150 cm, but contained no flint objects.

The house ruins outermost on the promontory were divided up into 2 groups, of which one, consisting of 2 almost round hollows with passage, were concealed in the fertile grassy slope, 20 m above sea level. The second group of 3 house ruins lay so near the strand that the high tide had eroded the midden slope in front of the site and had caused the passages and the houses' walling to collapse. The Eskimos' account that the land had sunk was confirmed, and it might even appear that the phenomenon is still valid.

Narssârssuk, 1953

Helicopter transport made a 4 day visit possible, 27–30th August, at Narssârssuk, 'the little plain', 18 km SW of Thule Airbase. The cliffy coast is interrupted here by a broad river mouth, surrounded by stony delta outwash at 3 different levels, and even further away from the river, of marine terraces. On both types of terraces a rich record of human presence over long periods of time can be found: house ruins, tent rings, graves, meat caches and fox traps. The most important discoveries at this site were the following:

1. A house ruin in the northern corner of the site, close to the strand, had its passage filled with sand, deposited at high tide as yet another proof of the sinking of the land.

2. In fertile vegetation at the foot of the marine terrace, behind the house ruin, a heavily decomposed musk ox cranium with attached horns was found, and close to the findspot under the moss a tent site was identified. The cranium is the 5th in a series of musk ox crania found in the Thule district south of Inglefield Land, and it is so far the only one that is in association with Eskimos' musk ox hunting. As the weight of a musk ox head inhibits long distance transport, it is probable that the animal was killed in the vicinity of the site.

The other 4 crania from the area are from a. the 'Pitufik', that is, the area around the current base, found by Qavigârssuak in 1947, b. 'The Fjord of the dead' 'De Dødes Fjord', by the route to the Inland Ice near Kap York, found by Odak 1948, c. 'Pingârssuit' mountain (now called 'P-Mountain'), near its summit, found in 1967 and d. The mountain over Uvdle on the south side of Wolstenholme Fjord.

3. On the 9-metre beach terrace, north of the house ruin, 5 tent rings were found, whose periphery stones were overgrown with read lichens and therefore so difficult to differentiate from the other stones on the terrace, that one could pass them without noticing them. No hearths were identified in or around the tent rings and in the terrain around were only very few, extremely eroded, bone splinters. At 50 metres distance from the rings a little harpoon head with open slot, of Thule type, was found.

4. Behind these tent rings two stone circles with closely aligned periphery stones were found, that were sunken into the terrain so that their surface protruded only few centimetres. One of these (figure 1.18), whose shape was an elongated ellipse measuring 280 × 130 cm in outermost dimensions, was oriented with its broad side towards the lake. The periphery stones were elongated but the south end was missing and there were flagstones in front. The other, 100 metres longer towards the NW, had rounded stones in its ellipse shaped periphery, which was missing at the front. The maximum dimensions were only 120 cm and it had

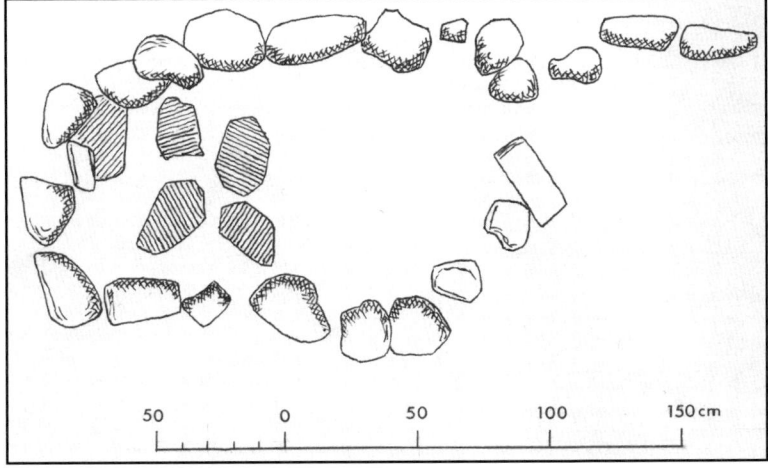

1.18
Tent ring from Narssarssuk 1953. Drawing E. Knuth

a flagstone floor. Close to the north end a hearth-like chamber was seen, consisting of three upright stones. None of the rings contained finds.

5. In the mountains behind Narssârssuk, 150–200 m over sea level, several examples of 'rows of stones for hare snares' were found. With 3–4 metres intervals stood one, two or three large upright stones, and between these stones or groups of stones, at a more or less regular interval, flat or round stones lay in the ground.

The first stone row that was seen had a length of around 100 metres and connected, with its meandering layout, a number of stone cairns, that resembled meat caches. Number 2 extended like a barrier, across a narrow gully where it connected a couple of walls of flat slate that were built on either side of the gully. In the lee of one of the walls a bedding structure was seen. The gully branched off to lead to a pass, whose sloped sides were connected by 2 parallel stone rows. Finally, on a mountain ridge over the gully, two stone rows were found, 10 metres apart, and one of these continued over a mountain top.

Holtved had observed this phenomenon west of the Umanak settlement site and I have seen it myself over the settlement site 'Lonesome Creek' in Conybeare Fjord, Grant Land, — the northernmost part of Ellesmere Island.

Head of Parker Snow Bay, 1958
A 2-hour visit with helicopter was made on 30 July. The bay is situated mainly west to east. At the landward end at the valley head (in Greenlandic 'qingua') are two valley glaciers flowing down from the Inland Ice, and the valley floor is cut by two rivers. North of the northernmost river in the NW corner of the valley, where the strand nears land at the foot of the mountains (inhabited by little auk), on the second lowest strand terrace lay a wooden hut, that apparently had been an Eskimo house. Behind this a couple of very fresh house ruins can be seen, and a number of tent sites and meat caches, that along with the hut must be the remains of the settlement 'Ivssugigssog' that according to Holtved housed 15 people in 1935.

The meat caches and possibly also some human burials lay between the rocks lowest on the land, from which a slope with abundant grass growth extended down over the house ruins. The tent rings lay partly at the foot of this slope, close to the south of the ruins, and partly on a series of strand terraces further away from the ruins, in the direction of the river. One of the rings in the former group looked as if it was divided by flat stones positioned on their edge in 2 rows, parallel to the strand. In a trial excavation between the rows of slabs bird bone and remains of wood were found, but no flint. The oldest looking tent ring in the group on the terrace lay c. 6 m over the strand and was completely overgrown with large-lobed dark lichen. It was very small and pear shaped, with a stone row across it as a partition between the innermost narrow area where the bedding had been and the broader floor space at the front.

South of the river, at a distance of 200 metres from the strand, and circa 30–35 m over the water level, lay a pair of bare gravel hills. In one of these <u>2 tent rings of the shelter type</u> were squeezed in side by side. They had rounded back walls, bedding partitions of thick long stones in a straight line and their width was 150–200 cm. In front of the ruins vertebra bones (of caribou?) and a little wood was found, but no flint.

In a mountain pass way up behind the qinqua valley in the direction of the northernmost glacier, the geologist <u>William E. Davies</u> found a hunter's bed.

Booth Sound, 1958
(76° 55 N., 71° 00' W.)
During the voyage by boat from <u>Hall Land</u> southwards through Nares Strait with the American ice breaker 'Atka' there arose the opportunity for a 1½ day visit at the site, where I was transported to land in the ship's Bell helicopter with tent and camping equipment on the 20th August at 6 o'clock in the morning.

Booth Sound lies in the middle of Steensby Land's outer coast formed as a 10 km wide and 5 km deep bay, that in its southern part sends a narrow fjord branching westwards. In the southwestern corner of the bay, close to the navigable passage from the sea, the 'Igánaq' mountain (Fitz Clarence Rock) sticks up like an island out of the water. In the northeastern corner a beautiful tongue shaped glacier runs down from Steensby Land's Inland Ice. I landed on a point south of the entrance to the above mentioned little fjord, close to 4 Eskimo houses, that were built a few years before by people from Qanâq and were put together with inferior quality wood. One of the houses was inhabited by <u>Jess</u> and family, another by <u>Maigssánguaq</u> and his wife <u>Avôrtúngiaq</u>, both of whom accompanied Holtved to <u>Inglefield Land</u> in 1936.

The survey, that, due to the short duration of the stay, was very superficial, and covered only sites in the large bay, and the fjord branch was not examined. Along the southern coast of the bay, and on the northern stretch from the mouth of the fjord to the glacier, terraces were found with apparently old tent rings, lying 5–10 metres above sea level, and overgrown with black large-lobed lichen. However, flint was not found at any of them.

The Eskimos Jess and Maigssánguaq put me in their rowing boat and sailed me past the glacier front, across the bay to the narrow land spit on the north side of the entrance. At the inner side of the land spit, where we landed the boat, is a steep cliffy coast, and the terrain on top, all the way out to the point, <u>Hoppner Point</u>, is covered in a confusion of large rocks. The space between these was extensively used for buildings of different types, dwellings of round or square shape, and meat caches with colossal stones for walling. Tent rings were also found, but in even the oldest looking and in those with the most dense lichen growth, rusty nails were found. In a crack in a cliff Maigssánguaq found parts of a toy sleigh of wood with bone shoes on the rails.

The peninsula south of the channel into Booth Sound, whose northern point is called <u>Blackwood Point</u>, was not examined. (Knuth 1977)

1.4 The Archaeology of New Nuulliit

1.4.1 New Nuulliit: Holtved's investigations

As mentioned earlier, Eigil Knuth's primary motivation for visiting Nuulliit was due to Holtved's studies and publications of the large Neo-Eskimo habitation at Nuulliit, and in particular the fact that Holtved did not have the time to excavate what he originally perceived as some of the oldest ruins (ruin group III). After some time at Nuulliit, while excavating in Holtved's ruin group III, Knuth found Palaeo-Eskimo evidence at a new location, and he therefore divided the archaeology of Nuulliit into 'Old Nuulliit' (The Palaeo-Eskimo habitations) and 'New Nuulliit' (The Neo-Eskimo habitations). These two groups are spatially separate at Nuulliit, both in terms of their location and their height above sea level.

On the outermost 'West Point' of Nuulliit, Erik Holtved discovered, in 1947, a large Neo-Eskimo settlement, consisting of 62 ruins (Holtved 1954). The settlement is situated on two low and narrow points, which run in a southeasterly direction parallel to the mainland. Forty-four of the ruins are defined as regular winter houses. The ruins were divided, by Holtved, into three groups, on both chronological and spatial parameters (see figure 1.19).

Ruin group I (ruin nos. 1–33) lies on the narrowest part of the point and is the most comprehensive group. Ruin group II (ruin nos. 34–46) is situated towards the mainland and consists of larger and obviously more recent ruins. Ruin group III (ruin nos. 47–51) lies about 300 m further inland. Holtved found that each ruin group represented a coherent habitation period. From excavations of group I, combined with relative dating of artefact inventory, and the architecture of group III, he deducted that these two groups were the oldest. However, he never managed to excavate ruin group III.

Absolute dating of musk ox horn from ruin 29, group I, was later conducted by Appelt (KIA-16936 and KIA-16941, dated to 884+/-25 BP and 724+/-20 BP). Thus Holtved's early relative dating of group I is confirmed by Appelt, dating ruin 29 to either the 12th or 13th century AD (Appelt 2003).

The ruins in group II were interpreted by Holtved as belonging to the late transitional period (the 16th century); however, they were never excavated, due to flooding of the site. Inughuit, living in Uummannaq, Thule, in 1947, also reused some of the group II ruins.

The settlement at Nuulliit was considered by Holtved as 'the largest hitherto known ruin site in Greenland', which is actually still true for the Neo-Eskimo

THE FIELD OF RESEARCH

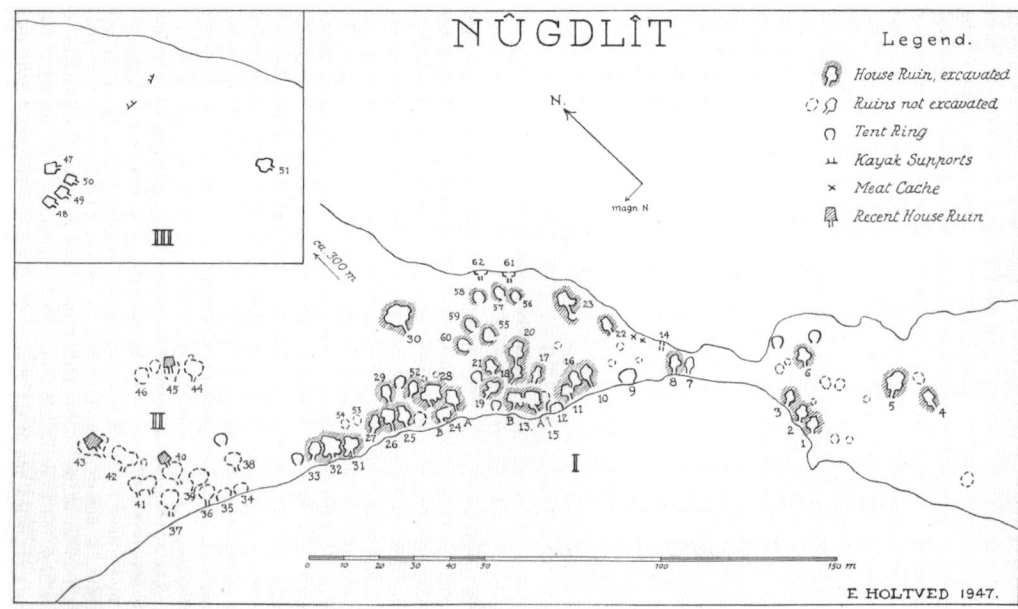

1.19 Map of the Thule winter houses at New Nuulliit by E. Holtved 1954

period. However, concerning the Palaeo-Eskimo period, the aggregation camp at Île de France, discovered by Knuth in northeast Greenland, far outnumbers Nuulliit (approximately 500 ruins are mapped) (Grønnow and Jensen 2003). The oldest ruins at New Nuulliit, group I, were intensively studied by Holtved, and from this ruin group a large collection of artefacts and information are kept at the National Museum of Denmark. Moreover, it can be concluded that 'New Nuulliit' has evidence of some of the earliest ruins and habitation by Thule Inuit in the Eastern Arctic.

1.4.2 Eigil Knuth's excavations of Thule culture ruins at 'New Nuulliit'

As earlier mentioned, Eigil Knuth's motivation for visiting Nuulliit was to excavate the shelter ruins, which Holtved left untouched (New Nuulliit group III). Knuth writes in his manuscript about his investigations of these ruins:

> The group lies, as previously mentioned, not on the narrow low point of 'West Point', where groups I and II are to be found, but 200 m towards the NE. As a result of their position in the terrain, the five ruins form two sub-groups, called group IIIa with the ruins

47, 48, 49 and 50 at the front end of the moraine, c. 5.5 m above sea level, and group IIIb, consisting of just ruin no. 51, on a significantly lower lying little rocky area, that must have been quite close to the coast, when the houses in group IIIa were inhabited.

The examinations, due to the conditions, could only be of a superficial nature, and they were limited thus to ruins 48 and 49 in group IIIa. As can be seen on Holtved's site plans, this group of ruins form a group where 48, 49 and 50 are situated beside each other with the entrances pointing towards the south (towards Wolstenholme Fjord) while 47 lies behind and above, with its entrance pointing east. The fact that the houses are built together means that a number of the walls could be used as walling and roof bearing components for two or even three of the houses.

Characteristic for the building style is the use of enormous stone slabs, placed as an inner lining, closely set beside each other, both in the square habitation areas, in the cooking annex and in the passages. These blocks were often of dimensions of over 100 cm in height and had sometimes a section of 40 × 50 cm. As many of them lay fallen into the middle of the floor, it took time and difficulty to manoeuvre them up onto the walling, using crowbars and wedges, before the excavation could begin.

Isolated large boulders, that apparently lay in situ as bedding supports, indicate that the bed has had a height of 40–50 cm over the floor level, similar to that which Holtved observed in the ruin group I no. 23. The large walling stones that made the living area and passages resemble the interiors of the Danish megaliths, and were the reason that the sun could never thaw the moss layer at the base of the ruins. After scraping off this layer it emerged that the cultural layers underneath, apart from at a few places in the passages and side chamber, were very limited.

After the discovery of 'Old Nûgdlît' it was necessary that all work should subsequently concentrate on this site. There was unfortunately no time left for the survey of the group IIIa ruins at 'New Nûgdlît'.

Ruin 48: On the floor consisting of stone slabs no finds were made, apart from a few bones. The annex chamber was placed in the west wall, just west of where the passage joined the house. On the floor just in front of the annex chamber lay a fresh looking bird leg with the webbing of the feet still preserved. The annex chamber was also tiled, and on top of its central tile was a thick cake of burnt blubber, but no stone lined hearth. The chamber floor was at the same level as the house floor and it contained the following: a number of bone fragments from baleen whale and baleen fibres, a soapstone fragment, a lamp wick trimmer and a baleen, bent and bound to form a cone, perhaps to be used as a ladle/scoop. The latter lay abutting the SW wall of the chamber, along with the remainder of the bird skeleton, from which the above mentioned bird leg came. No finds were made in the passage.

Ruin 49: Immediately east of no. 48. The floor in the main living area had only a few stone slabs and a very thin cultural layer with a few baleen whale fibres and bones. The annex chamber was, similarly to no. 48, placed in the ruin's SW corner and was placed such that it was wedged in, in front of no. 48's SE corner and passage. Up against the chamber's back wall was a very thick blubber layer, but there was no hearth structure. In the inner section of the passage the tip of a narwhale tooth was found, severely eroded. The floor in the outer part of the passage consisted of the natural bedrock, which at one place had a crack or a hollow with quite thick cultural layers. Here lay baleen whale string with knots and baleen whale fragments of up to 100 cm long and 10 cm wide. Some lay parallel with the passage walls, while others lay across the passage. In addition, finds included a flat axe or billet of whalebone with notch marks and a narrow distal slot, presumably for hafting an iron blade, a walrus rib bone, possibly used as a pressure tool, a flat limb bone of a musk ox (?), and a secondary shortened tension piece or kayak stud (figure 1.20).

THE FIELD OF RESEARCH

1.20 Ruin no. 49 in group III during excavation in 1958. Photo E. Knuth

Eigil Knuth's investigation of New Nuulliit ruin group III reveals three ruins (ruins 47, 48 and 49) as described by Holtved (1954). The three ruins are extremely well built using large stones, and Knuth compares them therefore to Scandinavian passage graves from the Neolithic Age. The architecture (oblong house plans with platforms and entrance in one end), as well as the findings inside the ruins (e.g. baleen artefacts, layers of bone and blubber and a possible kayak stud), reveal that the ruins belong to the Thule Culture, and probably not even its first part. Knuth's original hope and prime expectation – that these ruins belonged to the Palaeo-Eskimo period – was not met. One should expect that he was seriously disappointed, but he soon made a new discovery on the main cape. Knuth had, in addition to the investigations of ruin group III, been intensively surveying for Palaeo-Eskimo artefacts, at terraces on the main cape, and succeeded after a few days. He therefore continued his investigation on the main foreland on the site he termed Old Nuulliit.

2.0 The Archaeology of Old Nuulliit

2.1 Eigil Knuth's investigations of Old Nuulliit: ruins, artefacts and prehistoric traditions for each plateau

In the following text a description of the ruins at Old Nuulliit, their location, size, construction, excavation, inventory and possible cultural affiliation, interpreted on the basis of technology and typology, will be presented. The ruins are described systematically from plateau A to I, and are all labelled with a letter (A, B, C) referring to the plateau, followed by an individual sub-number (1, 2, 3, etc.) referring to the ruin. Descriptions of excavations and interpretations of the internal organization of the ruins are, if possible, cited directly from Eigil Knuth's manuscript.

2.1.1 Terminology and landscape

Eigil Knuth's conceptions and considerations concerning the landscape and his terminology of the archaeological site Old Nuulliit are well described in his manuscript in relation to his map of Old Nuulliit (figure 2.0) (Knuth 1977). He writes:

> The map (figure 2.0) shows, with the letters A, B, C, D, E, F, G, H, I, J and K, the terrain divisions that the area's topography and the Old Nûgdlît ruins' location seemed to indicate, gradually as the work progressed. The localities H and I contain 'Level II' ruins, and the ridge J between Lake II and Lake IV has apparently been uninhabited. All the other letters, in addition to their topographical reference, mark a ruin group belonging under Old Nûgdlît 'Level I'.
>
> When the author in the above lines speaks of the 'F-plateau' and its 'neighbour plateaus', he hides in the description 'plateau' his lack of expertise in the interpretation of the quaternary geological formation of the different stretches of land between the lakes and between the lake area and the sea. The characterising of the chaotic accumulation of stone boulders on the ridge K as moraine deposits on top of intrusive dolerite columns is the author's own

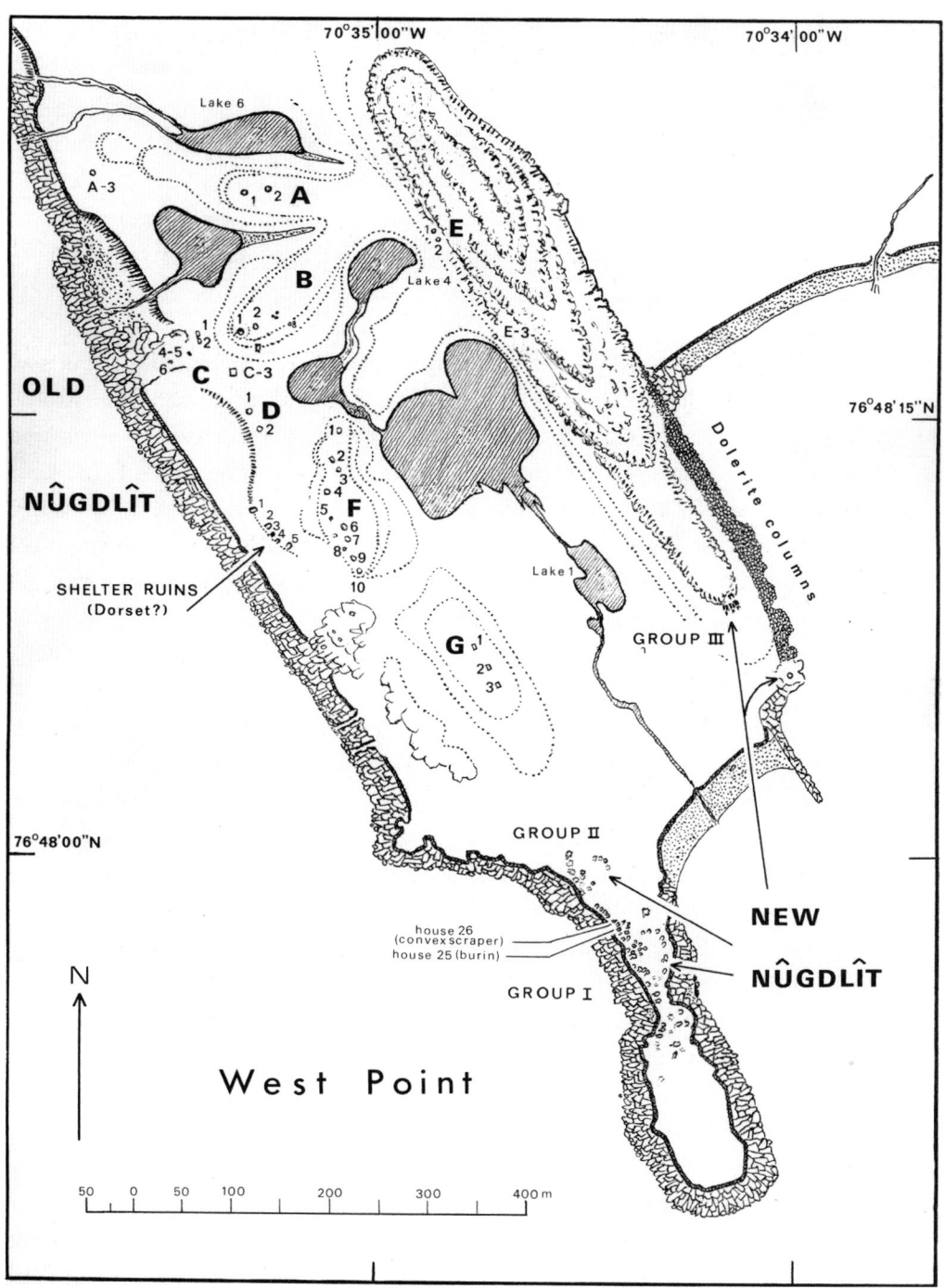

2.0 Map of the Nuulliit peninsula with its different ruin groups (I–III: New Nuulliit) and ruin plateaus (A–I: Old Nuulliit). (Knuth 1978)

interpretation, as is the assumption that the stony F-plateau, running parallel to K, contains a similar core of moraine formation, perhaps deriving from an advanced phase of the large glacier. Just north of the Nûgdlît peninsula, the gentle slope downwards from north to south of the F-plateau might be called a 'marine terrace'. The Stony ridge K falls on the southwest side in terrace-like levels down towards the lowland with the lakes 'Lake I' and 'Lake II' in the middle of the peninsula, and the same cliff terraces are distinct in K's extension to the northwest, where the ruin group E lies on one of the lowest terrace levels, down towards 'Lake IV'. The land spits A, B and J, between the different small lakes, extend like three spread fingers out from K and interrupt a surface of yellow-brown grass and pebbles. The A spit slopes gently from the K-ridge out towards the sea, and the persistent search for muscle shells on the surface of these three spits resulted in the finding of just two examples, both on B, but their presence can be due to birds, and does not allow the suggestion that these land spits have an underwater origin.

That the lowland between F and K once had been a bay must be seen as probable, but just for how long such a bay had existed here, while the ruin sites in Level I were uninhabited, is unknown. Considering that the spit of land at J has no ruins, it is possible that the earlier bay extended to the B-plateau, whereby it included the current extents of 'Lake III' and 'Lake IV', and gave not just the structures at plateaus G and F, but also the today so remote settlement at E, a connection to the sea. The peninsula would thus, with the southeast ends of G and K as points, appear with more or less the same outline as today, just with a shortened form.

Such reconstruction attempts with the aim of describing the Nûgdlît peninsula's 'archaeological topography', that is, drawing the structures on previously existing peninsulas or islands whose outline is based on the current differences in the levels of the terrain, can for many reasons be pure guesswork. Firstly, we cannot just assume that the existing ruins or ruin groups chronologically (or culturally) belong together, when the ^{14}C dates with their very large intervals say that they indeed do not. Secondly, we do not have, like in the Peary Land region, distinct evidence for the structures' relation to a continual land rise, where height over the current strand line is more or less proportional to the archaeological age.

In the Thule area the only definite information is the fact that over many generations, and probably over the last 100 years, the land can have undergone a land sinking in connection with a retreat of the glaciers. For Nûgdlît, periodic land rising and land sinking can have succeeded each other over the millennia that the dates that the ruins in Old Nûgdlît's Level I span. Finally, the identification of the ruins' absolute height in Old Nûgdlît contains inaccuracies, partly because of the heavy surf along the coast, and partly because of the great tide difference, that according to repeated measurements in 1975 seems to span 2.28 m at spring tide.

All in all, a quaternary definition of the Nûgdlît peninsula's terrain would unfortunately be impossible for an amateur to present. He can only record and relate the above described observations of the structural differences, at the sites on which the ruins were placed. (Knuth 1977)

As Eigil Knuth writes, the Old Nuulliit ruin group is situated north of the New Nuulliit Thule Eskimo ruins at the tip of the Nuulliit peninsula. The Old Nuulliit ruins are divided into groups on several secondary smaller fossil beach plateaus, often with lakes and lower lying landscape in between. Generally these ruins are difficult to recognize on the surface due to vegetation, sedimentation and boulder fields, and because the ruins themselves are light constructions. Knuth is uncertain about the isostatic Holocene movements at Nuulliit. However, it seems clear that the Palaeo-Eskimo habitations are lying at higher elevations than those from the later periods. It is also probable that the small lakes, which are now found on the plateau, formerly were bays and beaches so that the Palaeo-Eskimo ruins originally were placed on small coastal tombolos and promontories.

The ruins from plateau A to F, except plateau B, are situated from 8 to 11 m above sea level. These ruins are light constructions, characteristic of the early Palaeo-Eskimo traditions. At the lower lying plateaus, plateau B, G, H and I, the structures generally consist of more heavily built tent rings, shelter ruins and hunter's beds, typical of the Thule Culture. These ruins are generally referred to as houses.

2.1.2 The A-plateau

Ruin A-0, A-1 & A-2

The 'A-plateau' is situated approximately 10.5 m above sea level, and is the northernmost of the Palaeo-Eskimo ruin groups at Nuulliit. The ruins A1, A1b and A2 were intensively investigated by Eigil Knuth during the summer of 1975, and much of his original manuscript from 1977 is devoted to a description and interpretation of these ruins. In front of ruin A-1 an area (A-1b) consisting of fire cracked stones and dark soils, also yielding lithic artefacts, was perceived as an open air activity area used in connection with the tent ruin A-1. Ruin A0 was found in 1975 but was never further investigated. During the 1990 season, ruin A2 was re-examined and some more artefacts were recovered.

Knuth described the location of the A-plateau and its ruins as follows:

> The A-plateau's WNW-pointing land spit between Lake 5 and Lake 6 has already previously been compared to a finger, and it has, like a finger, two knuckles and a nail. If one wanders from the inner end of the finger, 'the main plateau', out towards the coast past ruins A-2 and A-1, you pass the middle knuckle in the form of a slightly higher arc-shaped stone bank, that is without doubt the apex of a previous point.
>
> The continued wandering in the direction of the sea brings you over the next part of the finger to yet another stone bank, possibly representing the apex of a point from a later period than the previous. Outside this finally lies the 'fingertip', with its outermost rounded stone bank, that forms the 'nail'. This short 'fingertip' rests on a terrace, running parallel to the outer coast at just over 9 m height above the current flood-tide sea level, and here lies ruin A-0, just south of the 'nail' and close to the slope down to the water's edge. (On the same terrace, that can be interpreted as an old beach, further to the SE, the ruin groups C and D are situated.)

Ruin A0

Ruin A-0 was discovered late during the 1975 fieldwork as a weak and somehow dubious feature estimated to be 4 × 4 m. This ruin was not excavated, and no artefacts were spotted by Eigil Knuth using his 'sun reflection technique'.

Ruin A1

Artefact no. LI.9856–69

Ruin A-1 is the westernmost of the ruins on the A-plateau, lying 10.40 m above sea level (high tide). It was discovered on 23 July 1975 as one of the few well-defined structures on the terraces (figure 2.1). Eigil Knuth was immediately able to find artefacts within the periphery. The ruin A1 consisted of a circular double periphery. The periphery was made of rocks, larger than the gravel on the terrace. In order to document the structure of the ruin, Knuth painted the outer stone periphery white, and then he started the excavation (figure 2.2).

2.1
Plateau with tent ring, ruin A before excavation. Photo E. Knuth

2.2
Ruin A1 after excavation. Periphery stones in construction are painted white. Photo E. Knuth

THE ARCHAEOLOGY OF OLD NUULLIIT

Inside the periphery, some areas were covered with grass, and Eigil Knuth suspected this vegetation to cover prehistoric fireplaces. The soil in these areas was black from charcoal, but no pieces were large enough for a conventional radiocarbon analysis. Several egg-shaped stones, found together inside the periphery, were interpreted as cooking stones. In the centre (figure 2.3: location J) some large fire cracked stones were found, and Knuth interpreted this feature as the main fireplace in the ruin. Secondary fireplaces and cooking areas were located at other places in the ruin (figure 2.3: A, H).

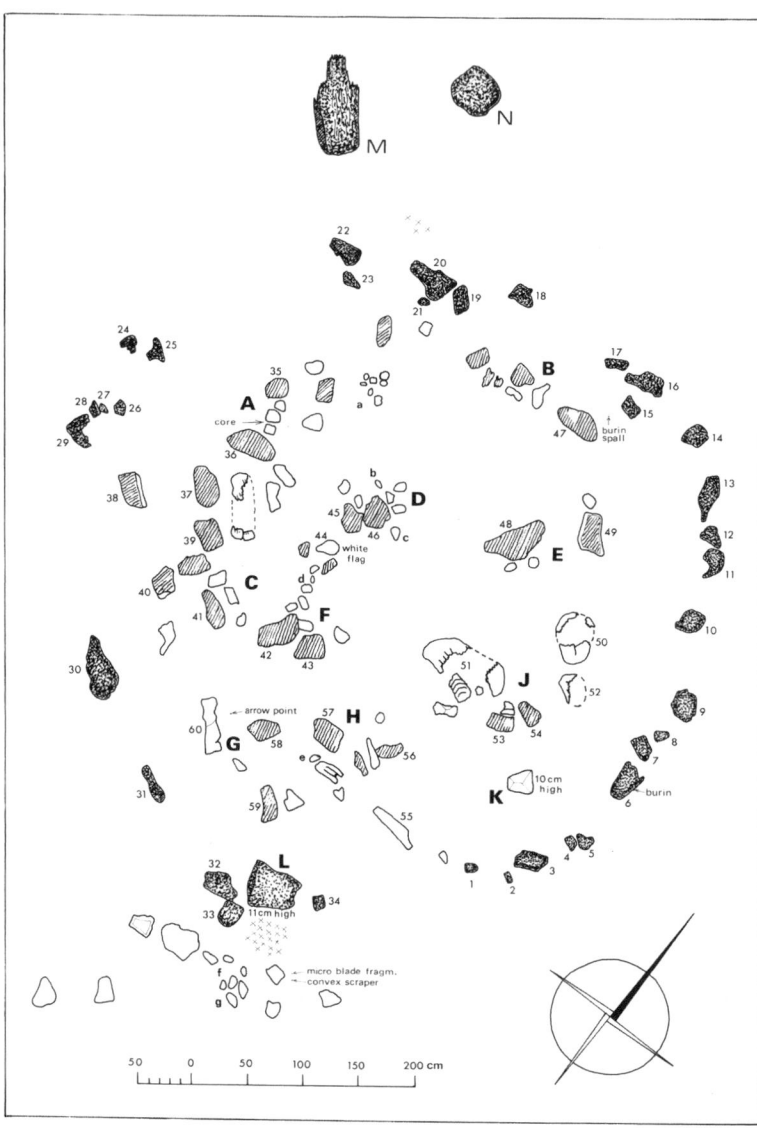

2.3
Plan of ruin A1 and A1b. Drawing H.C. Gulløv

When the ruin was excavated, the double periphery was still dominant as the ruin's main structure. Between the inner and the outer periphery, no fireplaces and only a few artefacts were found: a burin spall and some flakes. Outside the periphery, towards the north, a small concentration of flakes was found, possibly a dump. Two boulder-like stones (figure 2.3: M, N) were lying immediately north of the periphery, and Knuth suggested that these were used for wiring the tent, during the prevailing, stormy, northern winds – a problem Eigil Knuth and Erik Hoff were exposed to during the 1975 season.

Ruin A-1b
Artefact no. L1.9870–82
Outside the southern side of the periphery, beside a boulder (figure 2.3: L) and three small rocks, an area with 'suspicious' vegetation was found. During the days 22–26 August, this area was excavated. Beneath the vegetation, soil, black from burnt wood, and lithic artefacts were recovered. Moreover, a concentration of cooking stones was found here. Knuth interprets area A1b as an outdoor cooking place.

Ruin A1 and A1b and its organization
Eigil Knuth's interpretation of the ruin in his first manuscript from 1977:

The above description of A-1 has instinctively, between the lines, anticipated the conclusion that the ruin represents the remains of a tent dwelling, that is, the stone settings that a tent would have had, indoors and outdoors, at ground level.

It is pointed out that the ruin's inner core of flagstones (hatched in the plan) must be interpreted as a ring of hearths, even though, because of Nûgdlît's damp climate, well preserved charcoal fragments were not present. It has been mentioned also that the large boulders 'M' and 'N', towards Lake 6, can have served as anchors for tent stays. However the surest argument for considering A-1 as the ruin of a tent dwelling is in its marked outer ring of three-dimensional stones (numbered 1–31 on the plan).

They have been placed as weights, on the tent skins, around the base of the tent and have all rolled radially out when the camp was dismantled, and thus the sterility of the gravel in the space between these stones and the core periphery is explained. If we moved the stones back to the middle of this space, an original tent ring, in theory, emerges, of almost circular shape and with a diameter of c. 5.5 metres.

While we are never in doubt, when concerned with the Independence culture's ruins, about their layout and orientation, A-1 in this respect has no typical traits. In terms of the sloping of the ruin towards Lake 5, we should assume that the stone layouts 'A' and 'B' (the assumed seating arrangement) and the area between them mark the floor's innermost section, while the area from 'H' to 'K' marks its outermost. The boulders 'M' and 'N' would in that case be behind the tent, where one would usually want to be sure of the most secure tent-stay anchorage, the entrance would then be around stone 55 and the hearth area A-1,b would naturally be placed just to the right outside the door.

However there are other gaps in A-1's outer stone alignment, where the entrance can have been: between stones 22 and 25, or between 29 and 30, and both these positions would have allowed a view of the sea. The dwelling can, finally, have had an entrance from any direction, depending on the direction the wind blew. The question cannot be answered definitively, due to the following reasons: 1. We have no knowledge of the tent framing's construction, 2. in the floor's tiling we have no indication of the position of the entrance and 3. we are missing certain characteristics concerning A-1's age and the contemporary local topography.

Inventory, technology and tradition: ruins A1 & A1b
Ruin A1 (figure 2.4)
White-grey fine-grained mcq is used for the lithic production. Burin spalls (three specimens) clearly demonstrate that the inventory is part of an early Palaeo-Eskimo technology. However, the most significant indication of tradition in the lithic reduction process is a refitted micro blade core, refitted by Eigil Knuth from five pieces. The core was fractured due to natural (frost) cracks rather than to final reduction. The core has a fine facetted platform, is wedge shaped, single fronted and has a right angle between platform and front. This blade core morphology is, in Greenland, typical of the blade production in the Independence I tradition.

The rest of the lithic artefacts cannot be typologically attributed to any particular Palaeo-Eskimo tradition. Thus ruin A1 was probably used by an Independence I family.

2.4 Inventory from ruin A1. Photo J. Sørensen

Ruin area A
Ruin A1

Burin spalls	3
Bifacial preforms	1
Arrowhead preform	1
Micro blades	1
Micro blade cores	2
Flakes	90
Total	98

Ruin A1b (figure 2.5)
Eigil Knuth interpreted area A1b as an open-air workshop, related to ruin A1. The inventory from this ruin consists of artefact types such as burin spalls, scrapers

2.5 Inventory from ruin A1b. Photo J. Sørensen

Ruin area A
Ruin A1B

End scrapers	1
Side scrapers	1
Burin spalls	2
Bifacial preforms	2
Micro blades	2
Retouched pieces/other preforms	2
Flakes	43
Total	53

and some fragmented micro blades. A triangular end scraper has notches on both lateral edges and can be attributed to the Independence I tradition. The broad fragments of micro blades and the burin spalls support this attribution. Thus it can be concluded that artefacts from both A1-and A1b are made in an Independence I tradition.

Ruin A2
Artefact no. LI. 9883–9924, LI.10404–10490
Ruin A2 lies on the plateau 18.5 m east of A1 and 10.5 m above sea level (at high tide) (figure 2.6). Eigil Knuth excavated the ruin in 1975, from 6 to 14 August (figure 2.7). However, during this season, he never managed to measure and draw its layout, due to the bad weather conditions. He therefore returned to this ruin during the 1990 season to continue the excavation and finish the documentation (figure 2.8). Before the excavation started, the ruin appeared as a low depression into the gravel and only few larger stones were visible. The rest of the ruin was covered with lichens, mosses, grass, dryas and willow. The depression was circular and had a diameter of 5.6–6.0 m.

2.6
Plateau with tent ring, ruin A2, before excavation. Photo E. Knuth

THE ARCHAEOLOGY OF OLD NUULLIIT

2.7
Ruin A2 after excavation

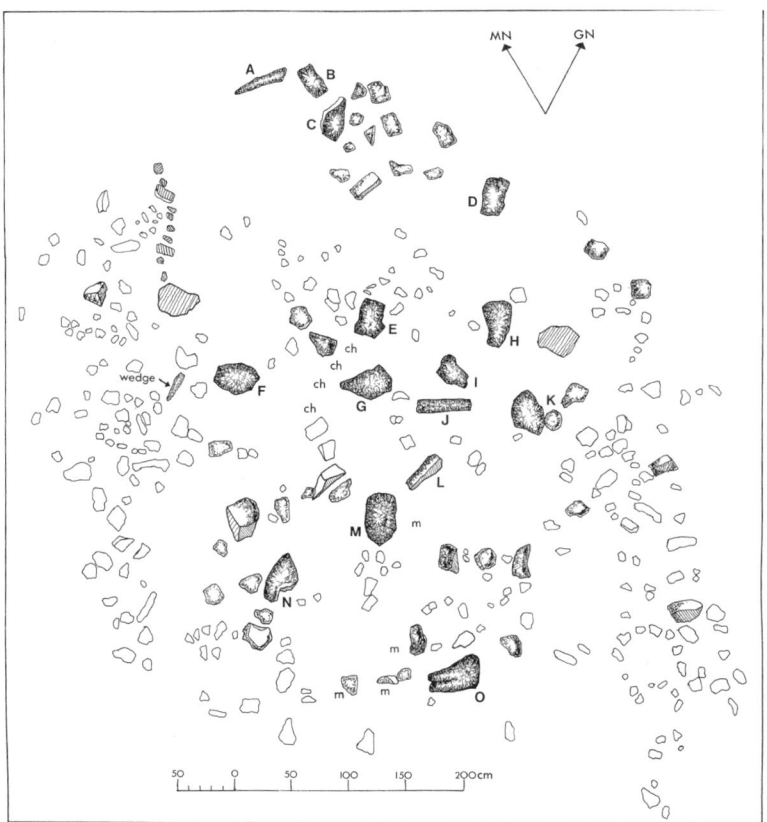

2.8
Plan of ruin A2. Drawing H.C. Gulløv

After excavation it appeared that the ruin had an even, horizontal floor, delineated by a circle of stones on its west and east side. The western periphery was built from hand-sized stones. The east-side periphery was narrow and built with smaller stones.

Inside the periphery many lithic artefacts were recovered, and the inventory soon became more comprehensive than at A1.

Like at A1, Knuth describes the internal organization of the ruin as extremely difficult to understand and he has a poetical passage in his 1977 manuscript about his struggles:

> As in the case of A-1, the interpretation of the layout and the orientation of the dwelling was problematic. One stood before an unknown phenomenon, an unfamiliar folk with unknown customs and 'language' and felt that one was in the same situation as the English aviator, Michael Ventris, when he wished to understand the Cretian script 'Linear B' without knowing which language is was related to. If I should be confronted with an Independence I or II ruin, I would never be in doubt as to how it should be tackled. I knew what I would come across and where; I would know the terms and the sentence construction. But here I had to be careful not to be lead by the Independence dialects when I used my excavating tools.

At one stage during the excavation, Eigil Knuth was tempted to interpret the internal organization as a former axial feature; however, he soon left this idea: the parallel stone lines were lying too far apart from each other. Moreover, what he perceived as the fireplace was not at all in the centre of the axial feature.

In the north-western interior, an area between some larger stones (figure 2.8: E, G, F) contained a great deal of charcoal and black earth. This area was perceived as a former central fireplace. Concerning the description of the southeastern part of the ruin, Knuth's own diary has some informative passages:

> 31/7-1975. Excavated in A-2, where the number of refuse chips increased from 93 to 105 pieces. West of the large almond-shaped stone (no. 26) exposed a little 'space' in which a willow (Salix arctica) was growing and which therefore, as I had experienced in Nûgdlît in 1960, could contain old bone material from which the willow roots drew nourishment. This proved to be correct. First, as a kind of forewarning, three of the apparently, for the

> site, characteristic symmetrical medial micro-blade fragments emerged. This followed with a couple of bone fragments (including L.1.9984) and right at the front end of the almond-shaped stone, at 8 cm depth, a fragment of a walrus tusk (L.1. 9983). It lay under and between the willow's root system and disintegrated on its surface when I removed it, but still could be removed intact enough that one could study how it was rounded by cutting at its broadest end.
>
> A couple of days later it happened again, that the removal of a little willow growth (at another place in the ruin) made a broad micro-blade fragment fly into the air. This time, it was a distal fragment of 1.29 cm width (L.1. 9908).

Eigil Knuth was thrilled by the fact that by locating willow and excavating the place where they grow, he was able to find ancient preserved bone material. A sea mammal bone from A2 was radiocarbon analysed in Copenhagen and obtained an age of 3770+/-50 BP. In his 1977 manuscript Knuth therefore poses the following question to his readers: 'Is it really possible that a bone of this age, still can spread nutrients to the soil?'

During the excavation of A2, Knuth makes what he certainly considers the most important single find in the 1975 season, and maybe in general, at Nuulliit. He writes:

> The greatest surprise that ruin A-2 had prepared for me came on 2 August 1975. I had excavated for hours in the north-western periphery of the ruin, without any finds except seven small chert chips and due to wind and rain was ready to go home to my tent. Nevertheless, I began, yet again, to examine the periphery to seek explanations for the still puzzling problem of the layout of the dwelling and its orientation.
>
> A little west of stone no. 10, a partly gravel covered, flat, wedge-shaped stone lay on the surface, which at its exposed end was spotted with the shiny silver lichen Rhizocarbon geographicum. I lifted it to see how long the end that was hidden under the gravel was and when I saw tool-marks in the, now exposed, pointed end, I turned it over. It thus turned out to be a well intact and very fine tool, an adze or a wedge, 27.5 centimetres in length (figure

2.9
Adze preform made from dolerite found in ruin A2. Photo J. Sørensen

2.9). The material was not chert, but limestone (dolomite). Its 5.63 cm wide front-end was sharpened into a narrow, flat edge by knapping on one surface. The butt was pointed, and the whole underside was trimmed, by removing large flakes but using a regular, well executed technique, while the upper, for the most part, was un-worked, except for the last 9.5 cm towards the sharp end, where trimming had been carried out on both surfaces. The underside had the apparently hard and fragile rock type's original dark, almost black colouration, while the lichen covered upper, due to the affects of the weather, was yellow-brown.

An object of such material and with such dimensions is not to be found, to the best part of my knowledge, in find descriptions in the Palaeo-Eskimo archaeological literature. At first glance, the axe, with its expertly executed rough knapping technique, stands out as a foreign element in the complex of Palaeo-Eskimo tool production, that has in some circles been given the collective term: the 'Arctic Small Tool tradition' (ASTt). It seems to be an intrusion from a whole other tradition, and a comparison of it to the miniature arrowhead L.1.7363 from ruin F-7 from 'Old Nûgdlît' gives us a strong impression of this.

Ruin A2 and its organization

Concerning the interpretation of the interior structure of ruin A2 Eigil Knuth writes:

> As it was indicated in the introduction to the discussion of ruin A-2 and repeated in the description of the excavation, this ruin did not tell us anything further about its layout and function than A-1 had done. On the contrary.
>
> Unlike A-1, it did not have a distinct stone ring that might be interpreted as the periphery of a tent-like dwelling. Before the excavation began it was thought that A-2's ring-shaped outer edge and the floor's vegetation cover was the ruin's periphery but this was found not to be the case. New stones and flagstones turned up everywhere and the result was a quite confusing collection of stones.
>
> A-2 presented us with the following information: to the west and east a form for delineation could be traced, in that at both places a curved alignment of stones was found. Along the west side this alignment consisted of fist-sized stones mixed with larger stones, while all the stones in the east side's alignment (that was narrower than that to the west) consisted of stones that were all smaller than those on the west side.
>
> On both the north (that faces 'Lake 6') and the south sides there were no periphery markings, but the floor surfaces' soil conditions both places were different. While the northern part, where the finds were very few, consisted of small stones with gravel underneath, the southern side had stone on top of stone.
>
> The quantity of chert implements and chips was significantly greater in A-2 than in A-1. If A-2 had been for human habitation with some form of roofing, it might have had a doorway either in the north or the south or, indeed, at both, in that one could choose to go in and out sometimes one way, sometimes the other, depending on the direction of the wind, just as my assistant and I, in 1975, had been forced to do.
>
> We have, in reality, no definite evidence that might support the view of A-2 as earlier flooring in a roofed dwelling, and any attempt to form a view of A-2 as a scene where a traditional division of domestic chores at specific locations, must remain guesswork.

Inventory, technology and tradition: ruin A2 (figure 2.10)
Ruin A2 includes a fairly large collection of lithic artefacts (240 pieces in all). All but one of the pieces are made from fine-grained, grey mcq. Many indications in this collection point to the probability that the tools were made by persons of the Independence I tradition. Firstly, the many specimens of broad micro blades point to this tradition; however, there are also flakes reduced in a four-sided reduction principle by means of indirect percussion. This technology is only described from Independence I in the eastern Arctic. Burins, burin spalls and an end scraper support this interpretation. The most peculiar artefact is the long, square sectioned axe preform, made from dolerite (and not dolomite as it is originally stated). The tool is delicately unifacially worked into a long wedge-shaped morphology along two nearly right-angled ridges. This artefact cannot be morphologically matched with other artefacts from the eastern Arctic. Eigil Knuth was thrilled by this 'tool' and described it thoroughly while also discussing its function as either a 'pick axe', an 'ice adze' or a 'wedge'. Moreover, he considered it an indication of a completely different culture at Nuulliit, comparing its uniqueness to the narrow arrowhead found in ruin F7. Thereby Knuth indirectly suggested that it could be of Denbigh origin.

2.10 Inventory from ruin A2. Photo J. Sørensen

Regarding the manufacture and technology of this tool, it is made by means of indirect percussion in a four-sided technology. This technology was used by the Independence I people, when thinning down tabular preforms, while at the same time producing flake blanks. Two arguments support the suggestion that the dolerite artefact was a preform for an adze head: 1) the Independence I tradition used indirect technique and squared reduction principles and 2) adze heads appear in Independence I, made from basalts, e.g. dolerite. The uniqueness of this artefact thus can be explained by the fact that it is so far the only adze-preform we know from the Independence I tradition.

It is interesting that no production waste was found from the manufacture of the adze preform from A2, nor from any other of the ruins at the site. In theory there could exist an adze workshop at Nuulliit if the dolerite is local. However, the fact that Eigil Knuth only found one perfect preform rather points to the fact that the preform was imported to Nuulliit and lost. The adze preform, though, raises the question of where large preforms of dolerite for adzes were produced during Independence I in north Greenland. The only other Independence I site with adzes in north Greenland is Pearylandville. Adzes are here made from a more dark and dense basalt.

Three bone fragments were found in A2. Eigil Knuth had two of them analysed by the zoologist Ulrik Møhl, who determined them to be from a large sea mammal, i.e. walrus or whale. The last bone has the shape of a pressure tool from Independence I. It was probably also made from a sea mammal. All the bones are in a bad state of preservation.

Ruin area A
Ruin A2

End scrapers	1
Burins	2
Burin spalls	13
Adze preform	1
Micro blades	16
Flakes	204
Bone material	3
Total	240

2.1.3 The B-plateau

Ruin B1

Ruin B1 is a large stone built feature made from large boulders and smaller stones. The feature was discovered and photographed in 1975, but was not excavated. This feature can be interpreted as a cache made by people of the Thule Culture (figure 2.11).

2.11 Ruin B1 at the B-plateau. Photo E. Knuth

Ruin B2

Ruin B2 is a stone-built feature, approximately circular and three metres in diameter. It is built mainly from head-sized boulders, but with some flagstones in the central part. The periphery of the feature is unevenly built, characterized by three

2.12
Ruin B2 after excavation in 1990.
Photo E. Knuth

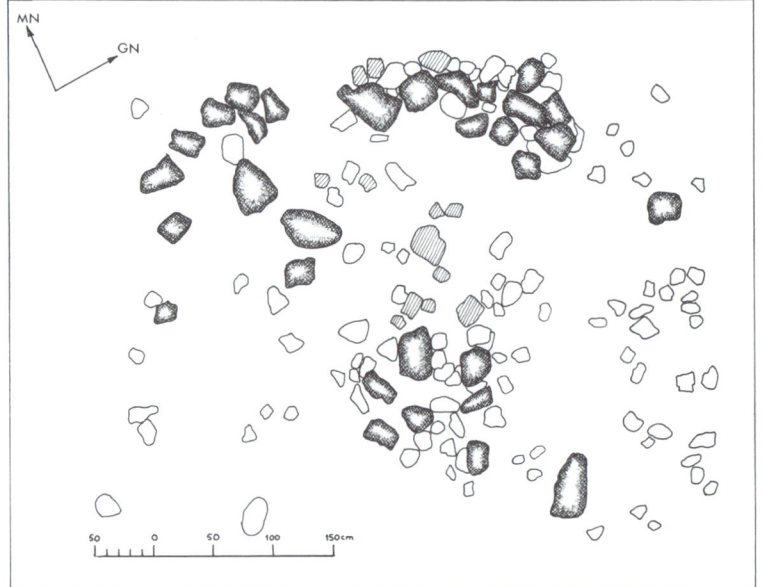

2.13
Plan of ruin B2.
Drawing
T. Grønnegaard

well-preserved 'wall constructions'. The northern wall is particularly strongly built, probably as a shelter from northerly winds. This ruin was found and photographed in 1975, and was excavated and drawn in 1990. No artefacts were found during the excavation. The ruin must be considered as the remnants of a tent construction, made by people of the Thule Culture (figures 2.12 & 2.13).

Ruins B6, B6 and B8
Ruins B6, B7 and B8 were discovered and photographed in 1975. They are close to each other but independent features, well built from head-sized boulders. The walls of the features were easily spotted on the surface. In 1990 the three features were excavated and drawn (figures 2.14 & 2.15). The shapes of the features are circular with a distinct entrance on one side and platform edges centrally through two of the features. However, these features are surprisingly small, generally only 1½ × 2 m, which means that the platforms generally only cover one square metre. During excavation no artefacts were found. The architecture of the features is typical of the Thule Culture, and the features must be interpreted as shelters for short-term use, raised during special (weather) conditions by Thule people. No fireplaces or artefacts were found associated with the features.

2.14 Ruin B6-8 after excavation in 1990. Photo E. Knuth

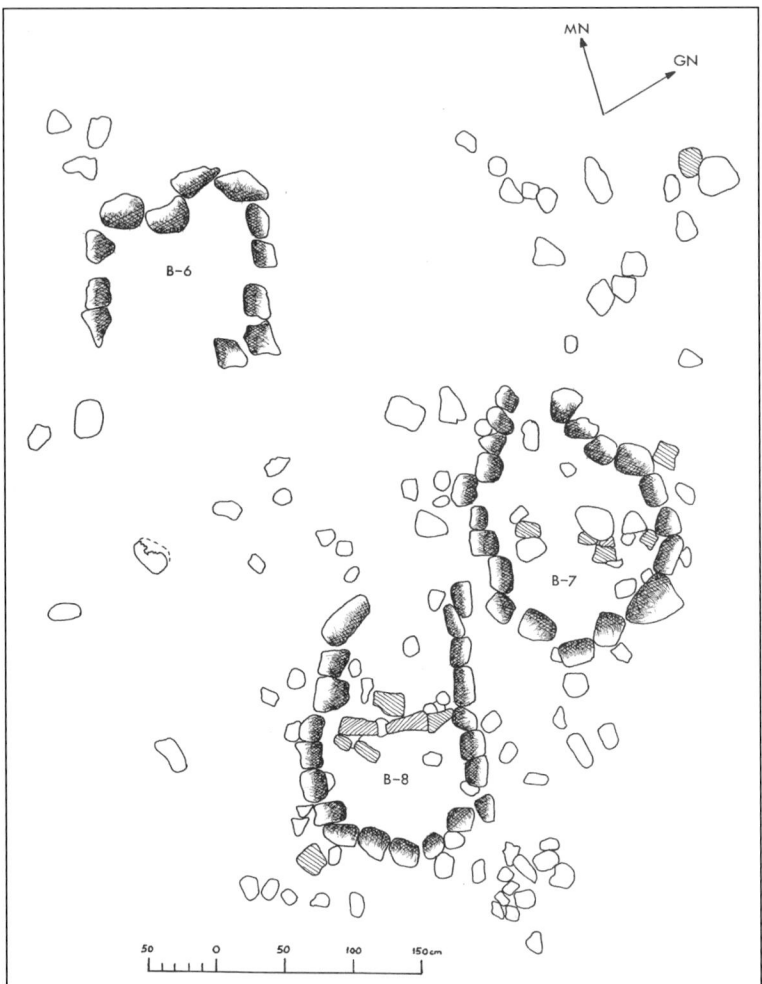

2.15
Plan of Ruin B6-8. Drawing T. Grønnegaard

2.1.4. The C-plateau

Ruin C1

Artefact no. LI.9925–28

Ruin C1 is a circular ruin, approximately 4 m in diameter (figures 2.16 & 2.17). The periphery is built mainly of head-sized and hand-sized stone slabs. The wall is well built of closely placed stones, and there seems to be an entrance passage towards the south. Close to the centre, a fireplace, in the form of a pavement of hand-size stone slabs and containing charcoal, was situated (figure 2.18). A small amount of charcoal was collected and brought to the National Museum during the 1990 season. The ruin was discovered in 1975 and was thoroughly excavated and drawn in 1990. Inside the ruin lithic artefacts were found. The spatial distribution of the lithics seems to reflect a working area between the fireplace and the entrance. Almost no artefacts were found in the northern part of the ruin. Thus this area could well have functioned as the platform and sleeping section. The architecture of the ruin

2.16
Ruin C1 before excavation.
Photo E. Knuth

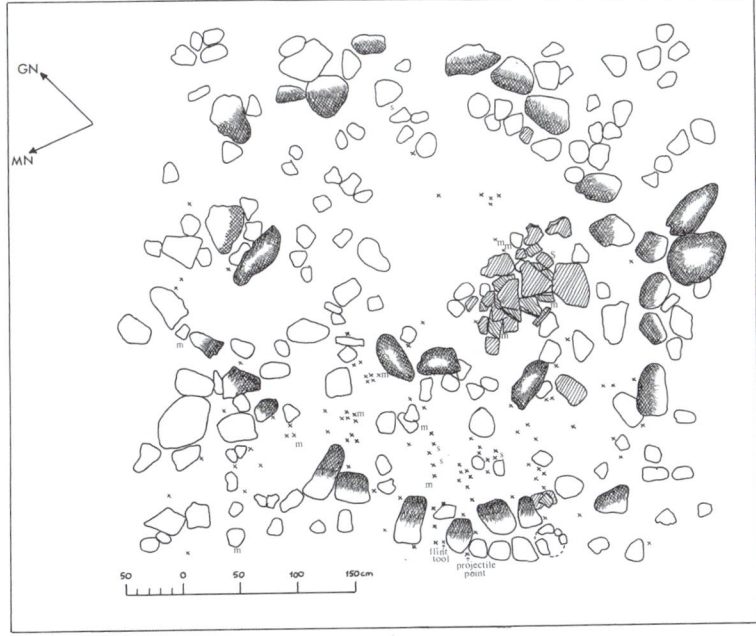

2.17
Plan of ruin C1.
Drawing
T. Grønnegaard

2.18 A fireplace in Ruin C1 excavated in 1990. From this fireplace charcoal of local wood was sampled for later ^{14}C dating (KIA 32917). Photo E. Knuth

and the selection of stones for the construction (generally slabs) are characteristic of the early Palaeo-Eskimo tradition. The intensive production of lithic material supports this interpretation. Generally the ruin seems undisturbed and, considering the spatial layout, only used during a single occupation.

Inventory, technology and tradition: ruin C1 (figure 2.19)
Ruin C1 includes a technological, homogeneous inventory yielding artefacts from blade production, burin rejuvenation and bifacial production processes. The inventory in all the ruins on the C-plateau is characterized by the same grey mcq as is also known at the A-plateau. Burin spalls attribute the ruin to the early Palaeo-Eskimo period. The blade industry, which consists of a blade production of fairly wide blades (up to 11 mm in width), is typical of the Independence I blade technology. An AMS dating was run as part of the re-analysis of Old Nuulliit. The dating was made on charcoal of local willow twigs from the central fireplace and produced the date 3674 +/- 40 uncal. BP (2135–1979 cal. BC). Thus the date corresponds with the late phase of Independence I in the High Arctic (Grønnow and Jensen 2003).

2.19 Inventory from ruin C1. Photo J. Sørensen

Ruin area C
Ruin C1

Burin spalls	3
Arrowhead preform	1
Arrowhead	1
Micro blades	10
Retouched pieces/other preforms	1
Flakes	110
Total	126

Ruin C2
Artefact no. LI.9929–34, LI.10514–19

Ruin C2 was discovered and partly excavated in 1975 (figure 2.20). However, it was not finished before the 1990 season. This feature must also be considered as a former tent dwelling, but it is more oval in its shape than C1. It measures approximately 4 × 2 m. Ruin C2 has a well-preserved wall construction towards the north, built mainly of slabs. Towards the south the wall is uneven but characterized by

2.20
Ruin C2 during excavation in 1975. Photo E. Knuth

2.21
Ruin C2 after excavation in 1990. Photo E. Knuth

a few large, maybe naturally situated boulders, which could have been part of the construction. A presumed entrance is situated in the southern wall. Centrally, across the ruin, a weakly marked mid-passage, built of many small stone slabs, is situated. No fireplace is related to it.

Inside the structure some lithics were found generally structured as clusters centrally on the western side of the presumed mid-passage (in all 47 pieces). However, since the ruin was excavated during two seasons and probably not spatially mapped in 1975, it is not certain how complete this distribution pattern is. The architecture and the inventory of this ruin suggest that it was in use during the early Palaeo-Eskimo period.

Inventory, technology and tradition: ruin C2 (figure 2.2)
Ruin C2 includes, in its inventory, a complete arrowhead and an exceptionally long primary burin spall. Blade production seems not to have been carried out at this location. Some large flake blanks and flake preforms suggest that tabular cores were worked by indirect technique. The technology carried out at C2 can thus be attributed to the Independence I.

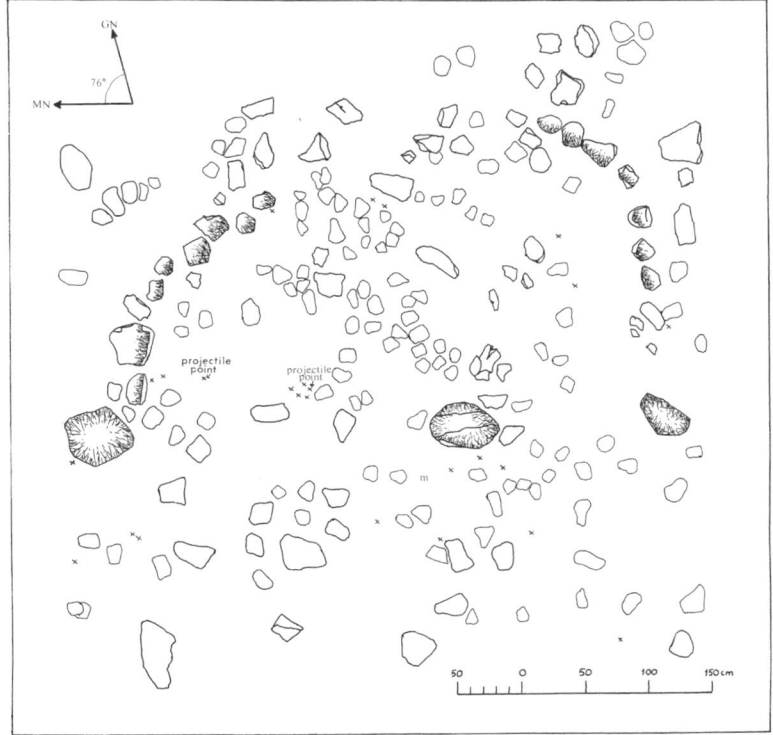

2.22
Plan of ruin C2.
Drawing
T. Grønnegaard

2.23 Inventory from ruin C2. Photo J. Sørensen

Ruin area C
Ruin C2

Burin spalls	2
Arrowhead	2
Micro blade	2
Retouched pieces/other preforms	3
Flakes	40
Total	49

Ruin C3
Artefact no. LI.9935–45
Ruin C3 is a circular tent ring. It was, like C2, discovered in 1975 but completely excavated and mapped during the 1990 season (figures 2.24 & 2.25). Photographs of the ruin, taken during the excavation, display a layout which is quite difficult to

understand, since the surface is covered with stone slabs. However, from the final drawing after the excavation, both architecture and artefact distribution seem to make sense. A periphery, approximately 3–3½ m in diameter, was built by many large stone slabs. Inside the ruin more stone slabs form a presumed fireplace, maybe as part of a mid-passage structure. Outside the periphery to the north a large boulder is situated, and Knuth's interpretation was that this could have been used as an anchor for tying the tent construction in case of strong northerly winds. The tent ring is generally solid except towards the north, where an entrance probably was situated. In his drawing Knuth has put a sign of a tent pole together with a question mark at the eastern and western side of the tent walls. The signs are connected with stone-built foundations. Thus Knuth's interpretation was that a tent was erected on these foundations.

A good number of lithics were found during excavation (142 pieces). The spatial distribution of the lithics is very specific: nearly all lithics are concentrated

2.24
Ruin C3 during excavation in 1975. Photo E. Knuth

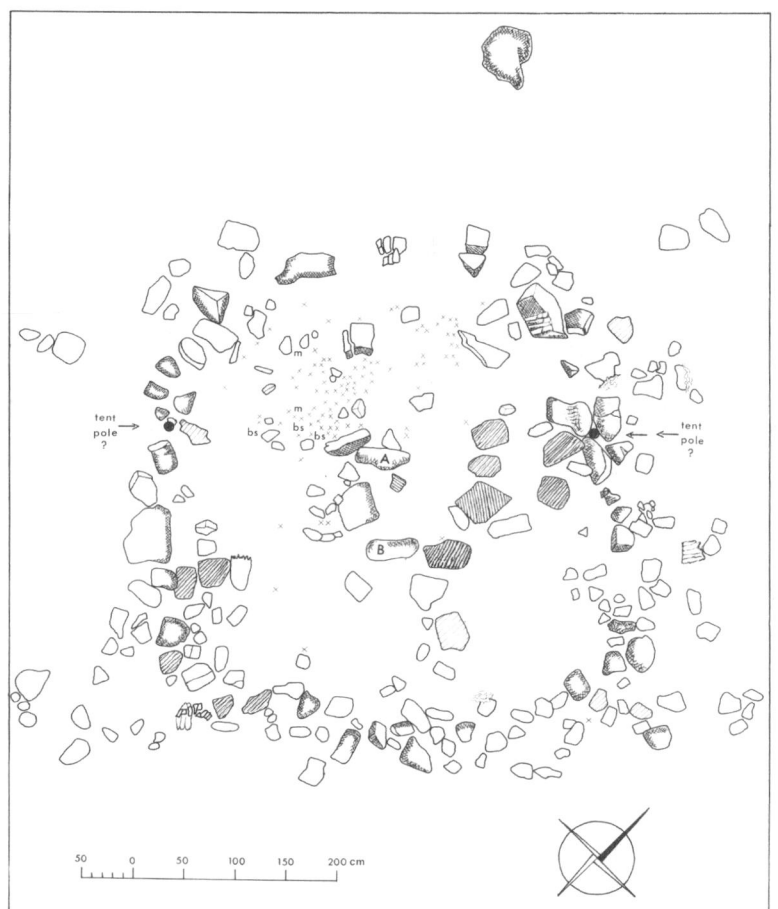

2.25
Plan of ruin C3.
Drawing H.C.
Gulløv

in the northern section, between the entrance and the central feature. Thus the workshop area must have been situated here, opposite to a sleeping area situated towards the south. A similar spatial pattern was seen in ruin C1. Due to its clear spatial pattern and limited but specific artefact inventory it seems possible that this ruin was used during only one, rather short, occupation episode.

Inventory, technology and tradition: ruin C3 (figure 2.26)
Ruin C3 has an inventory typical of an early Palaeo-Eskimo tradition characterized by a minute bifacial production, rejuvenation of burins by spalling, and a preform for a triangular harpoon end blade. Only one (medial) blade fragment (9 mm in width), probably a remnant from re-tooling, was found. The inventory from this ruin cannot be related to a specific tradition, but it is typical of Independence I, and Pre-Dorset.

THE ARCHAEOLOGY OF OLD NUULLIIT

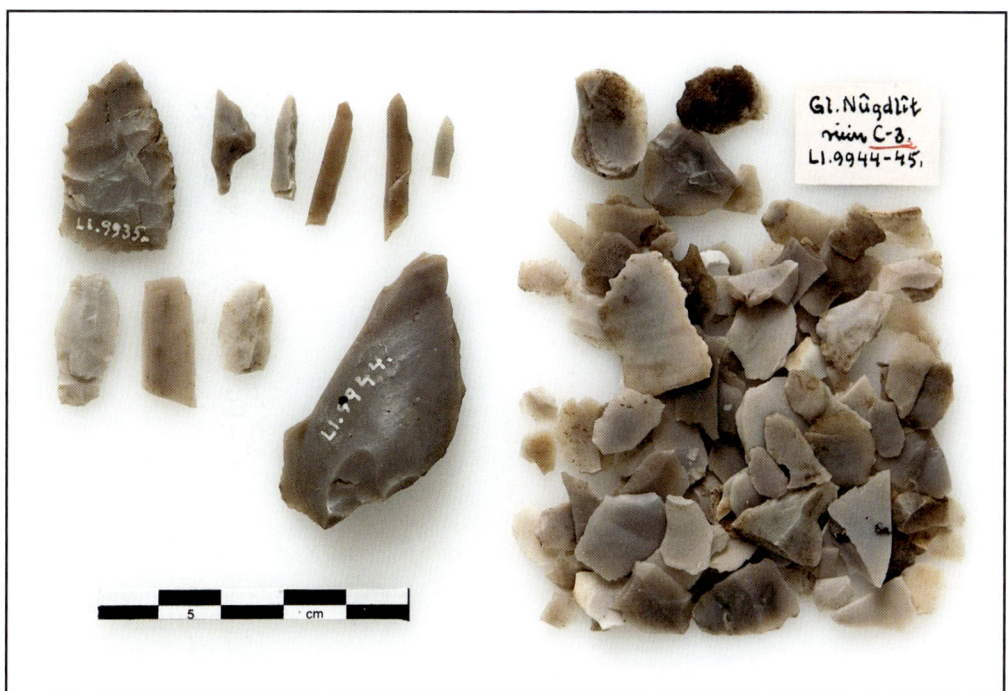

2.26 Inventory from ruin C3. Photo J. Sørensen

Ruin area C
Ruin C3

Burin spalls	4
Harpoon end blade preform	1
Micro blades	2
Flakes	135
Bone material	1
Total	143

Ruin C4

Ruin C4 is a small, dense feature built from head-size boulders. A single photo from 1975 is the only documentation of the ruin. This feature is most likely a cache. Its cultural affiliation is unknown, but it seems reasonable that the feature belongs to the habitation at the C-plateau (figure 2.27)

2.27 Ruin C4. Photo E. Knuth

Ruin C5
Ruin C5 is, like C4, a dense feature built from large boulders, only registered by a photograph (in 1975) (figure 2.28). The feature probably also served as a cache. Its cultural affiliation is unknown.

Conclusion on lithic inventory and tradition at the C-plateau
The ruins at the C-plateau are generally homogeneous in inventory sizes and raw materials and they represent unmixed technologies. Characteristic for the technology is a production of relatively broad micro blades and true burins. It is thus possible that the three tent rings and the two caches belong to a contemporary Independence I settlement phase.

2.28 Ruin C5. Photo E. Knuth

2.1.5 The D-plateau

The D-plateau is situated about 10 m above sea level, 100 m southeast of the A-plateau and close to the sea. The concentration of dryas is dense at this plateau and Eigil Knuth had great problems finding the ruins at the D-plateau, probably due to the vegetation. He writes:

> To illustrate the invisibility of the ruins it might be mentioned that I, at the site on 29 July 1960, at 9 or 10 o'clock at night, collected 150 small fragments of flint waste, and it was not until later, when the sun was lower, that I discovered that all of these flint fragments were concentrated within the boundary of a tent foundation (about D1, in manuscript from 1977).

Ruin D1
Artefact no. LI.7338–41

The ruin D1 lies 10.20 m above sea level. It is the northernmost of the ruins. It has an oval periphery measuring 3.70 m and 3.30 m across. The ruin is situated at the coast. An opening in the stone oval towards the sea (SW) is probably a former entrance. The floor inside the periphery consisted of gravel partially covered by dryas (figures 2.29 & 2.30).

Inside the ruin two different fireplaces and a pit were excavated. Eigil Knuth considered the first fireplace as the 'normal type for Nuulliit' consisting of an irregular stone pavement. This fireplace is placed centrally, but closer to the 'back wall' (i.e. away from the entrance). The second fireplace was situated just to the right of the entrance, as seen from in front of the structure. This fireplace is described as being in a niche and as quite large. In front of the central fireplace a cooking pit built from small stones was found. Inside the periphery the floor layer consisted of humus and an ash-like substance with a yellowish colour. Knuth states that the yellowish colour could well derive from deteriorated bones.

2.29
Ruin D1.
Photo E. Knuth

2.30
Plan of ruin D1.
Drawing
H.C. Gulløv

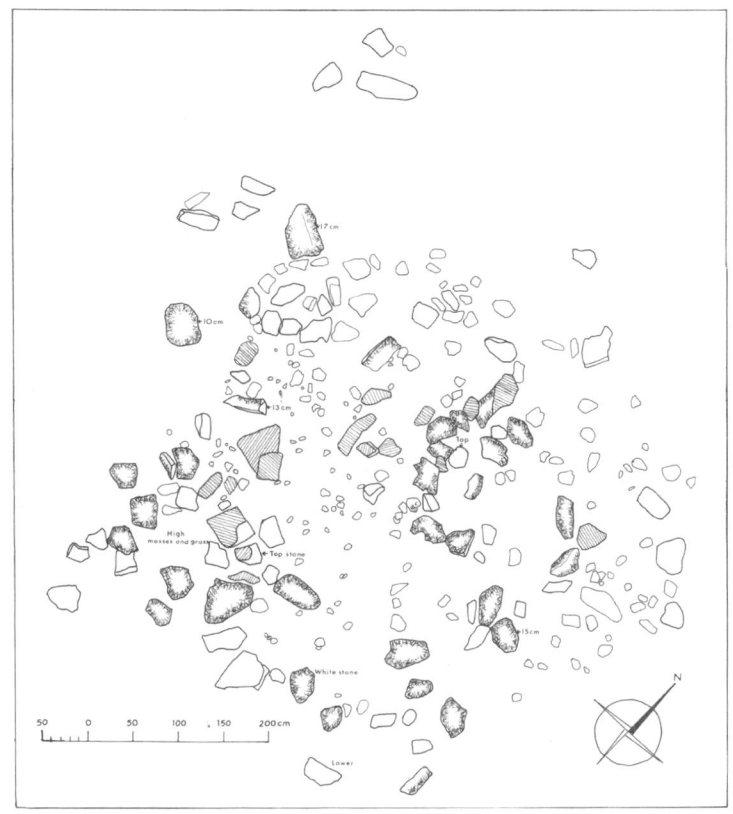

The ruin was constructed of stones. Two column-like stones of basalt, with a length of 45 cm each, were part of the construction in the north wall. The distance between these two stones, when erected, would have been 155 cm. In the west wall, towards the sea, a compact wall construction had been established consisting of 5–6 large stones placed closed together. The periphery of the ruin was thus more solid than other ruins at Nuulliit, but the stones were generally not erected, as on the ruins on the 8.5 m plateau. Flakes and debris were found scattered inside the ruin.

Inventory, technology and tradition: ruin D1 (figure 2.31)
Ruin D1 has a very low frequency of tools and rejuvenations compared to flakes and debris (tools, flakes and debris = 799; rejuvenations = 19). All worked lithic material is made from the grey mcq. Tools and rejuvenations consist of one burin and 13 burin spalls. Moreover, only three fragments of micro blades are found. The burin has a broken distal end, but it is a typical simple burin, only rejuvenated by spalling. The large amounts of flakes and debris consist mainly of small bifacial flakes, probably produced by direct soft percussion. However, there are also a few

larger flakes produced from tabular cores by means of indirect technique. At least one large biface was probably produced during occupation of D1. The many examples of rejuvenations of burins also suggest that bone material was worked intensively. The broad blade fragments, the burin technology and the general reduction indicates that the dwelling was used by Palaeo-Eskimos from the Independence I tradition.

2.31 Inventory from ruin D1. Photo M. Sørensen

Ruin area D
Ruin D1

Burins	1
Burin spalls	13
Micro blades	3
Retouched pieces/other preforms	2
Flakes	799
Total	818

THE ARCHAEOLOGY OF OLD NUULLIIT

Ruin D2
Artefact no. LI.10520–22
Ruin D2 was discovered in 1975 on the D-plateau. It was a ruin which was extremely difficult to separate from the subsoil, since the ground, like the ruin, consisted of many slabs and boulders. The ruin was carefully excavated and drawn in 1990 (figures 2.32 & 2.33). There is a central circular area cleared of stones, but with

2.32
Ruin D2 after excavation in 1990. Photo E. Knuth

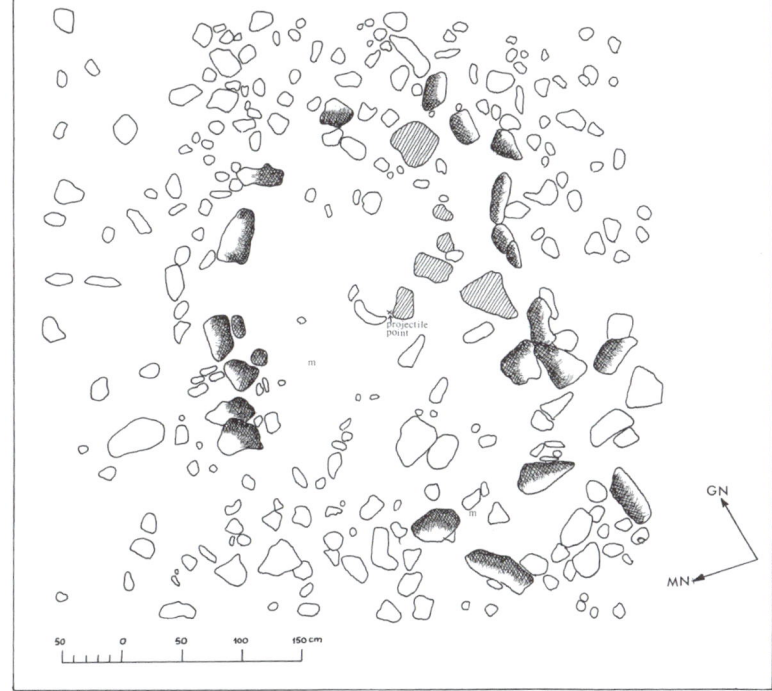

2.33
Plan of ruin D2. Drawing T. Grønnegaard

some selected slabs inside. A tent ring is built mainly from large stone slabs, but with many smaller slabs around. The size of the ring is approximately 2½ m in diameter and it seems to have been circular. Due to its architecture, spatial layout and small amount of lithic inventory, the ruin was probably only used during a short stay.

Inventory, technology and tradition: ruin D2 (figure 2.34)
The ruin D2 inventory consists of only three artefacts, all made from grey mcq: a burin, a distal fragment of a micro blade and a small flake. The burin is a com-

2.34
Inventory from ruin D2. Photo J. Sørensen

Ruin area D
Ruin D2

Burins	1
Micro blades	1
Flakes	1
Total	3

pletely used up simple burin, rejuvenated only by spalling. The burin is typical of the Independence I tradition, but could in principle also derive from an early Pre-Dorset context. From a technological point of view, it seems probable that both excavated ruins on the D-plateau were used by people of the Independence I tradition.

2.1.6 The E-plateau

Ruin E2
Artefact no. LI.9966–72
Ruin E2 was discovered in 1975, as a complex of large boulders on the gravel terrace. The boulders were lying in a somewhat circular shape approximately 2 m in diameter. Knuth excavated this feature in 1975 (figure 2.35). Centrally in the feature several small slabs were situated close together, possibly as part of a former fireplace. During excavation, Knuth discovered a fairly large collection of lithic debris (405 pieces), but no diagnostic pieces or tool types were among these. In 1990, the feature was measured and drawn (figure 2.36). The feature seems built in

2.35
Ruin E2 during excavation in 1975. Photo E. Knuth

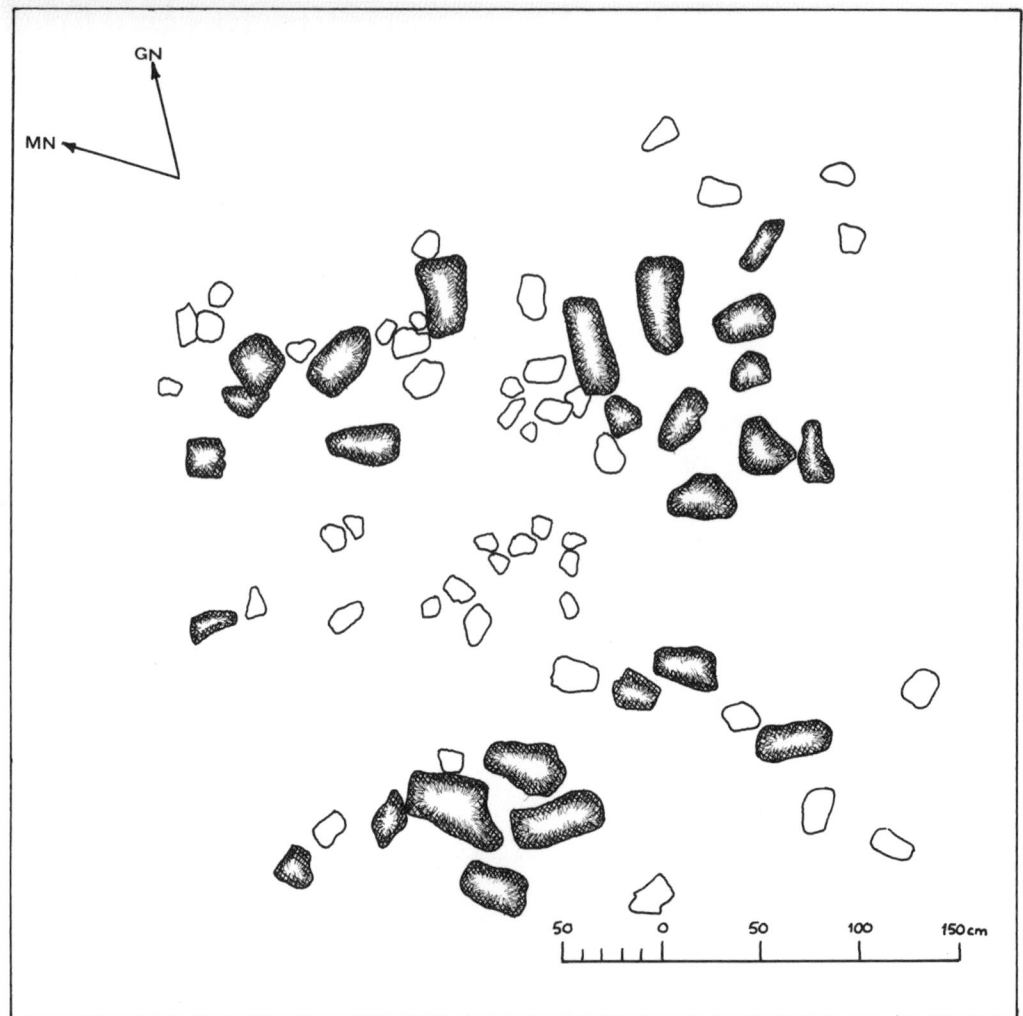

2.36 Plan of ruin E2. Drawing T. Grønnegaard

a hurry and it probably represents a former light tent construction with an internal fireplace. The lack of lithic tools and preforms in the inventory suggests that the tent was only used shortly, and that only a single lithic blank was exploited and exported from the ruin as a tool or preform.

Inventory, technology and tradition: ruin E2 (figure 2.37)
Ruin E2 contains an inventory of 405 flakes, generally smaller than 1 cm. No cores, rejuvenations or tools are present. The flakes are typical bifacial flake types. Some flakes have an outer layer of white chalk-like cortex. It is suggested that at least one

large bifacial tool was produced at E2. The bifacial technology cannot be culturally attributed.

2.37 Inventory from ruin E2. Photo J. Sørensen

Ruin area E
Ruin E2

Burin spalls	1
Flakes	404
Total	405

Ruin E3
Ruin E3 is a well-built tent ring made from fairly large boulders and slabs. The only registration of this ruin is a photo from 1975 (figure 2.38). From the photo it can be seen that the feature is circular and that it might contain a mid-passage. However, the large construction could also be interpreted as an indication of Thule culture architecture.

2.38
Ruin E3. Photo
E. Knuth

2.1.7 The F-plateau

The F-plateau is the southernmost of the plateaus containing Palaeo-Eskimo habitations. The plateau has the shape of a ridge, lying north – south. The ruins are lying as pearls on a string along this ridge. In total, Knuth located twelve ruins here, and he numbered them in sequence from north to south (figure 2.39).

Ruin F1
Artefact no. LI.7342–43, LI.9973
Ruin F1 is situated at the north-eastern corner of the F-plateau. The ruin appeared as a 'summer tent' due to the fact that it was built from only few stones, placed at

some distance in the periphery. The floor inside the ruin was flat and made even with gravel. The ruin was not excavated, but a surface collecting was made.

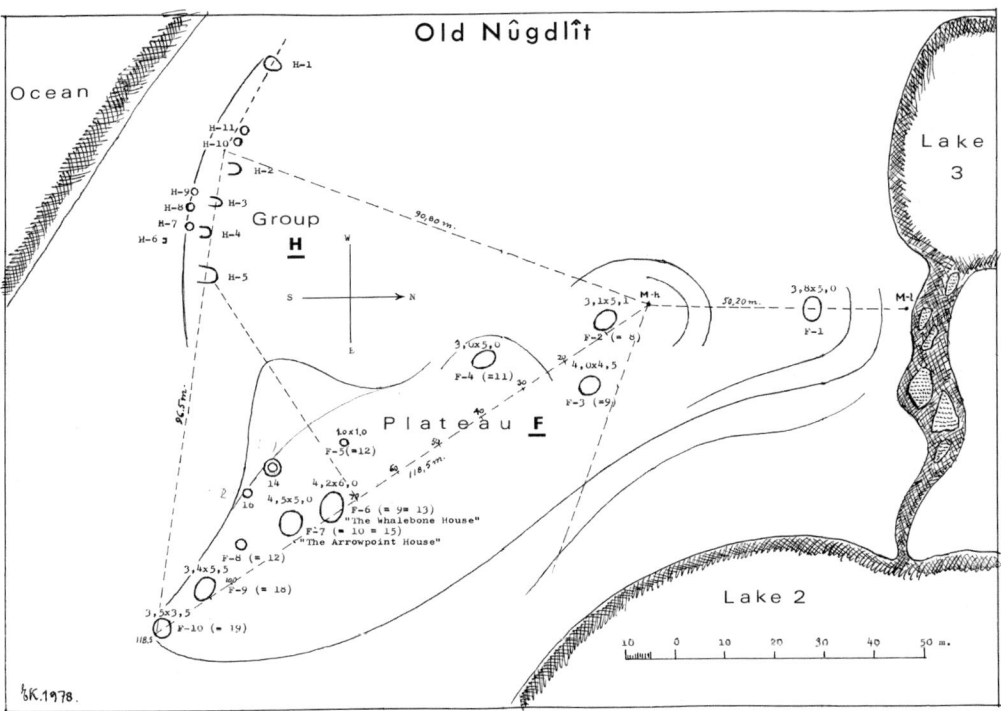

2.39 Plan of the F-plateau with ruins. Drawing E. Knuth 1978

Inventory, technology and tradition: ruin F1 (figure 2.40)
Ruin F1 has only few flakes in its inventory. They are, as in all the ruins at the F-plateau, made from fine-grained grey mcq. Generally the flakes seem to derive from a bifacial process. However, the few flakes are unequal in size, and do not reflect one representative technological process. This can be explained by the fact that the lithics were surface collected. Thus the lithic process in the ruin cannot be completely described. It is not possible to suggest any particular cultural affiliation or tradition based on the lithic artefacts.

Ruin area F
Ruin F1

Flakes	30

2.40 Inventory from Ruin F1. Photo M. Sørensen

Ruin F2
Artefact no. LI.7346
Ruin F2 is placed at the highest place on the P-plateau, approximately 11.50 m above sea level, and about 80 m south of ruin D1. About 10 m west of the ruin a 'fugleudkigssten' (i.e. a rock favoured by birds) is standing, overgrown with read lichens, and with grass in front (figures 2.41 & 2.42).

2.41
Ruin F2 before excavation.
Photo E. Knuth

2.42
Plan of ruin F2.
Drawing
T. Grønnegaard

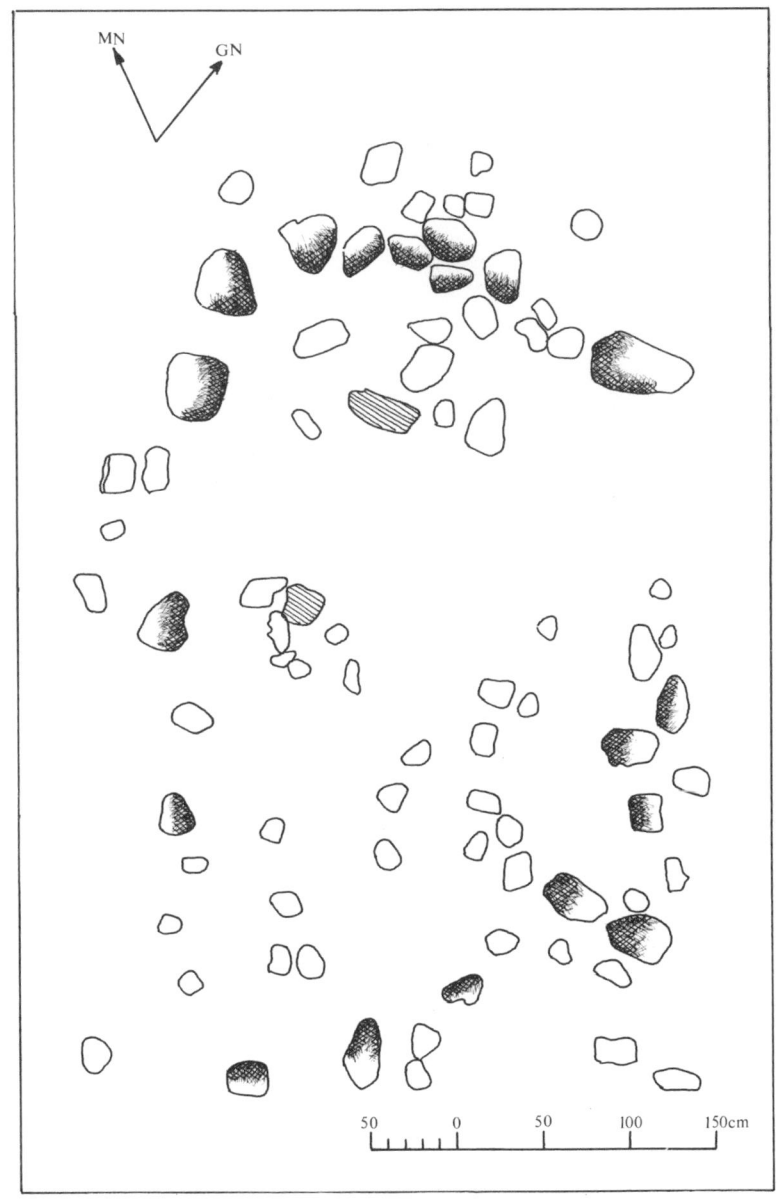

Inventory, technology and tradition: ruin F2 (figure 2.43)
Ruin F2 has, like F1, a small technologically heterogeneous assemblage, consisting of flakes of different sizes. No diagnostic lithic artefacts were found.

2.43
Inventory from ruin F2. Photo J. Sørensen

Ruin area F
Ruin F2

| Flakes | 10 |

Ruin F3
Artefact no. LI.7344–45, LI.9974
The ruin F3 was very difficult for Eigil Knuth to separate from the natural surface of the terrace. It consisted of several rows of stones forming a periphery (figure 2.44). The ruin was situated 5–6 m south of ruin F2. This ruin was located in 1958. On the surface, inside the ruin, a distal part of a burin and 23 flakes were found. An excavation was started in 1960, but was not completed due to lack of findings.

2.44 Ruin F3 during excavation in 1960. Photo E. Knuth

Inventory, technology and tradition: ruin F3 (figure 2.45)
Ruin F3 resembles ruins F1 and F2, in terms of the lithic inventory: only a small amount of flakes in different sizes are present. At least some of these derive from a bifacial reduction, or bifacial rejuvenation. However, in this ruin, the distal end of a simple burin with a spalled edge was also found. The burin is made with a minimum of effort from a flake blank, and is typical of an early Palaeo-Eskimo tradition: Independence I or Pre-Dorset.

Ruin area F
Ruin F3

Burins	1
Flakes	22
Total	23

THE ARCHAEOLOGY OF OLD NUULLIIT

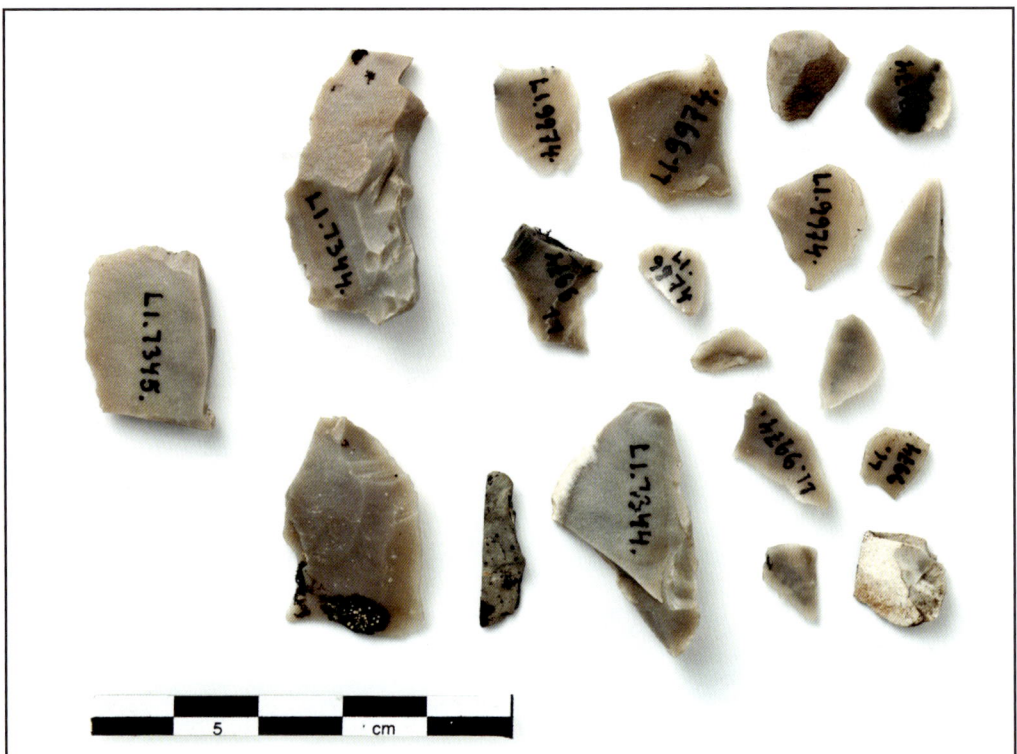

2.45 Inventory from ruin F3. Photo J. Sørensen

Ruin F4
Artefact no. LI. 7347–57
Ruin F4 is situated at the highest part of the F-plateau, approximately 11.40 m above sea level, only a short distance southwest of ruin F3. The ruin was completely excavated in 1960 (figure 2.46) and drawn in 1990 (figure 2.47). The periphery of the ruin could not, even after the excavation, be determined with certainty. However, judging from the cultural layer the outline of the ruin was oval and its long sides were situated along Lake 2. The size of the ruin was approximately 3.7 × 3.3 m.

The entrance in the periphery was indicated in the south west corner as a narrow opening made like a small path. Ruin F4 had a compact wall construction in the northwest corner, made from 5–6 close lying stones. Just inside where Knuth suggests an entrance, a fireplace was situated. This fireplace was not stone built. The cultural layer near the fireplace and a few other places in the ruin was as deep as 30 cm.

Outside the ruin a burin spall was found. Inside the ruin an atypical, thick-sided scraper with a convex edge was found, as well as several other lithic artefacts. Moreover, a piece of walrus tusk was excavated.

2.46
Ruin F4, 30 years after excavation. Photo E. Knuth

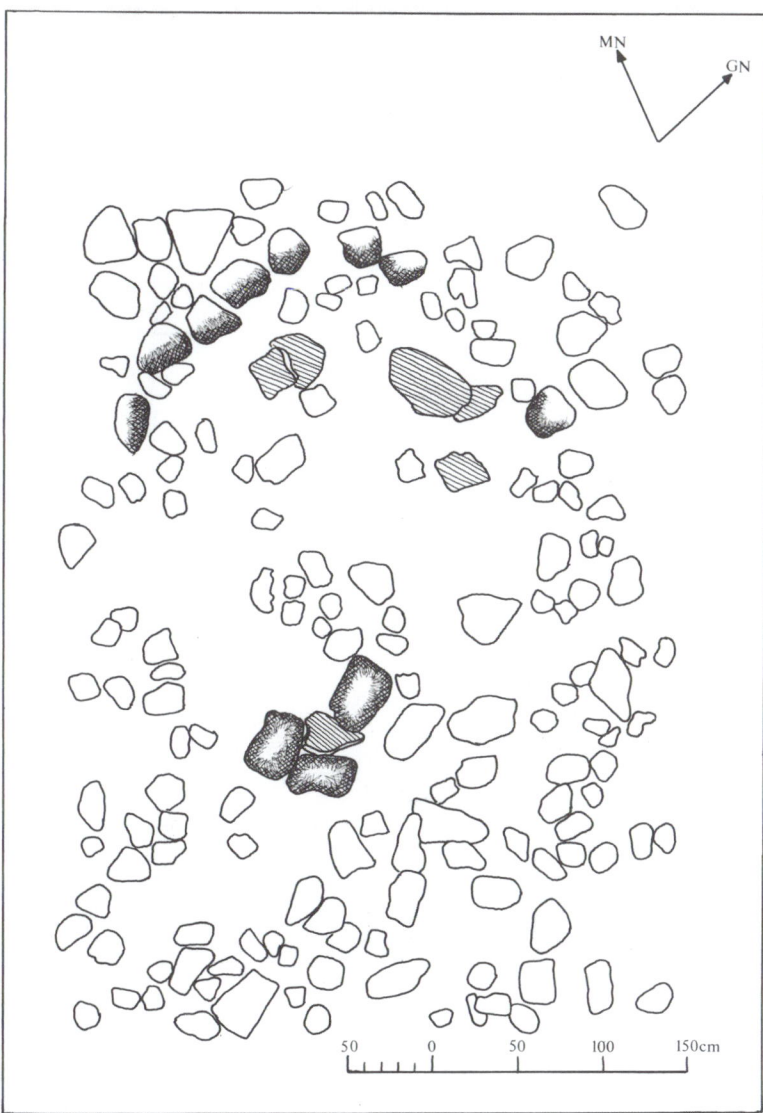

2.47
Plan of ruin F4. Drawing T. Grønnegaard

Inventory, technology and tradition: ruin F4 (figure 2.48)
Ruin F4 was, unlike the previous mentioned ruins at the F-plateau, excavated. The inventory consists of a burin and three burin spalls, a side scraper with a convex edge, some blades, and a small amount of small flakes from bifacial production.

2.48
Inventory from ruin F4. Photo M. Sørensen

Ruin area F
Ruin F4

Side scrapers	1
Burins	1
Burin spalls	3
Micro blades	3
Flakes	13
Bone material	2
Total	23

The burin is morphologically rather atypically 'S' shaped, but can be characterized as a simple burin with a spalled edge. The burin edge is rejuvenated by a series of small retouch flakes from the burin edge onto the distal face of the burin. This is a rejuvenation technology that is typical of the Pre-Dorset tradition. The blade production consists of regular prismatic blades, skilfully manufactured by pressure. The width of the blades is maximum 7 mm, and therefore leaves the impression of a narrower blade industry than at e.g. the A or D plateau. The side scraper with the convex edge is atypical but may appear in Pre-Dorset collections. To summarize: the lithic technology at ruin F4 points to the fact that people from the Pre-Dorset tradition inhabited this feature.

Ruin F5
Ruin F5 is situated 34 steps south of ruin F4. The ruin appeared as a tent ring with the front against the sea. The ruin measured 3 × 3 m. In front of the ruin a cache made from stones was situated. The ruin was not excavated and no findings were made in relation to it.

Ruin F6
Artefact no. LI.7358–60, LI.9975–79
This ruin was situated 15 m southeast of ruin F12 and approximately 50 m south of ruin F4. It was excavated in 1960 (figure 2.49) and drawn in 1990 (figure 2.50). It consisted of a large stone-built periphery of oval outline. The pointed end of the oval was situated towards southeast, and its long side was situated parallel to the coastline. It measured 3.00 × 4.25 m. Few stones of different sizes, lying in a double

2.49
Ruin F6, 30 years after excavation. Photo E. Knuth

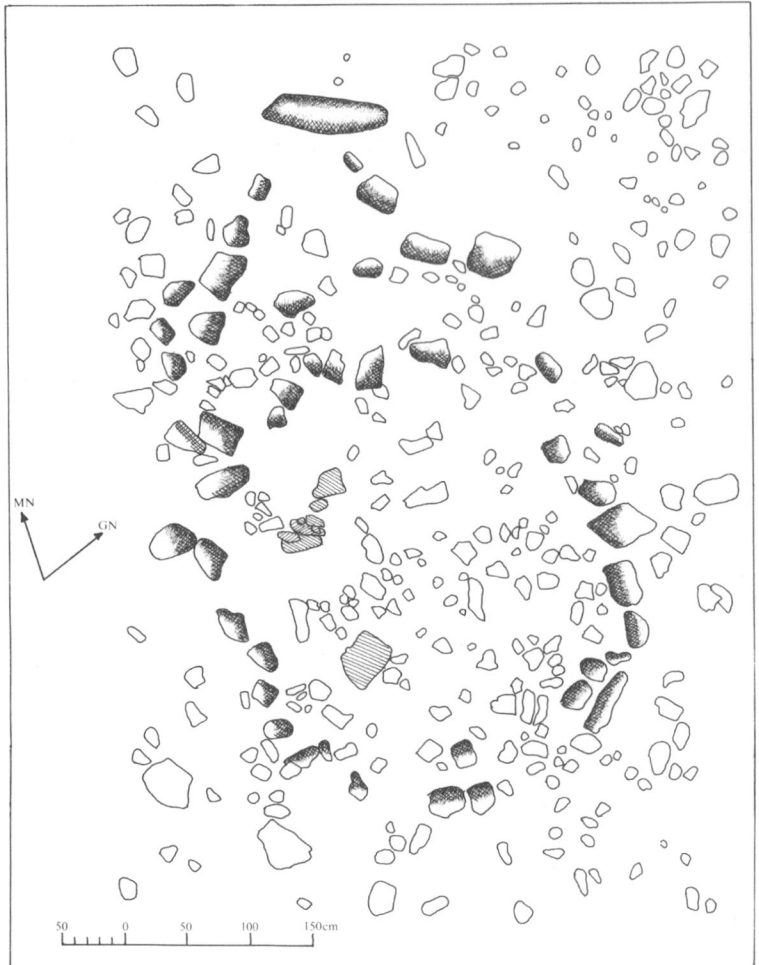

2.50
Plan of ruin F6.
Drawing
T. Grønnegaard

periphery, marked the periphery. The stones in the periphery were generally lying deep in the gravel and therefore hard to separate from naturally deposited stones at the terrace. The ruin was excavated. Across the floor, a little closer to the front wall than to the back wall, a single row of primarily flat stones was found. Behind the middle of this stone line, a white stone slab with traces of fire was lying. A layer of ashes was found here too.

In the western side of the floor, in front of the stone line, a circular pit, 40 cm in diameter, built from three stones, was found. The pit contained ashes and could thus have been used for cooking.

As an exception on the F-plateau, a small arctic willow (Salix arctica) was growing inside ruin F6. The explanation for the small willow shrub came when it was removed: a root pulled up pieces of whalebone from the gravel. Eigil Knuth refitted the whalebone into a 29.2 × 6.65 × 1.65 cm sized piece. The whalebone was later analysed at the radiocarbon laboratory in Copenhagen. It was dated to an absolute age of 4500+/-110 uncal. BP (K-1628), which is an unrealistic early date due to the marine reservoir effect. However, Knuth was partly using this date as an argument for a very early habitation at Nuulliit. A little east of the white stone slab a deteriorated bone tool, presumably a harpoon head, was found.

Inventory, technology and tradition: ruin F6 (figure 2.51)
Even though this ruin was excavated it produced very little lithic material. The only formal tool type is a thin triangular harpoon end blade, broken at the basal corner. The lithic harpoon end blade is morphologically typical of the Independence I and Pre-Dorset traditions. Flakes from F6 are fairly large and uneven, suggesting that small debris was not recovered during the excavation due to lack of sieving.

2.51
Inventory from ruin F6. Photo J. Sørensen

Ruin area F
Ruin F6

Harpoon end blade	1
Retouched pieces/other preforms	1
Flakes	5
Bone material	1
Total	8

Ruin F7
Artefact no. LI.7361–68, LI.9980

Ruin F7 was situated on the middle of the F-plateau. It was excavated and drawn in 1960 (figures 2.52 & 2.53). It appeared as a large well-built oval periphery, with its long side parallel to the coast. The size of the ruin (internal measurements) was 4.20 × 3.50 m. A broad path, made from stones and flagstones in a variety of sizes, appeared across the floor, parallel to the axis of the oval. This pavement separated the floor into a northwestern and a southeastern area.

2.52 Ruin F7 after excavation in 1960. Photo E. Knuth

The excavation of the ruin was carried out during the 1960 season, and the floor inside the ruin was completely excavated. It appeared that the pavement covered a fireplace dug into the gravel, 25–30 cm below the floor layer. The outline of the fireplace seemed to be defined by a number of fragments of 'dolerite columns' with a length of 35–45 cm. The overall interpretation by Knuth is that the pavement is a part of a mid-passage structure with a central box hearth, as known from Independence sites in Peary Land.

Below the left side of the mid-passage pavement a deeper lying pavement was found (figure 2.53: L). Around this pavement ashes appeared, and flags in the pavement were for some reason littered with a chalk-like material. In front of the mid-passage pavement, under a presumably tilted flagstone, another ash pit was found. Finally an ash pit was found in the northern corner of the southeastern floor area.

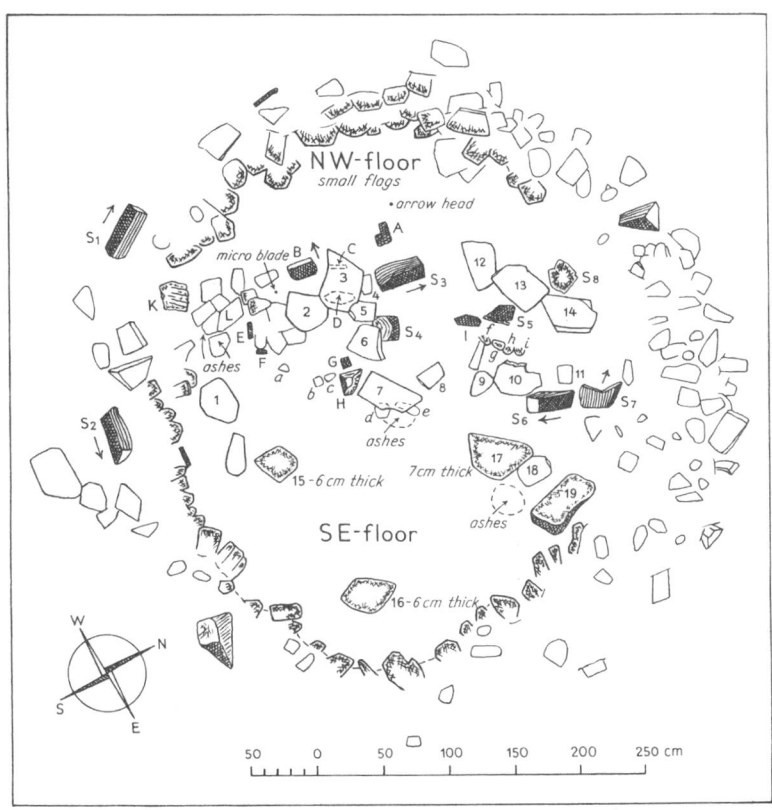

2.53
Plan of Ruin F7.
Drawing
H.C. Gulløv

The entrance could not be determined with certainty, but Knuth argues that it had been at the end of the mid-passage pavement, because: 1) most of the ruins have their entrances in this direction and 2) outside this supposed entrance a foundation appeared, which is typical of other mid-passage ruins from Peary Land.

Among Eigil Knuth's most important findings from the ruin were a stemmed end blade, that he surface collected, in as early as 1958, and a very narrow and delicate arrowhead, excavated from the northwestern floor area in 1960.

Inventory, technology and tradition: ruin F7 (figure 2.54)
Ruin F7 has, in its lithic inventory, two artefacts which have been the main reason

2.54 Inventory from ruin F7. Photo J. Sørensen

2.55
The arrowhead from ruin F7 is 2.8 cm long.
Photo J. Sørensen

for Knuth's persisting interest in Nuulliit, and the cause of his later field seasons. The most mysterious of these is a very slender arrowhead made with an outstanding finish in the detail (figure 2.55). Indeed, Eigil Knuth was right that this piece, in its style and technology, is different from arrowheads (he had seen) in Greenland, i.e. in Independence I and Saqqaq. The other lithic artefact that kept Knuth busy was a large complete stemmed end blade, found already during his first season of fieldwork. He compares this tool, with good reason, to similar artefacts from Independence II, or what we today term Greenlandic Dorset. When reinvestigating the inventory, the broken base of another stemmed end blade was discovered. Moreover, the inventory yielded a narrow prismatic micro blade, two burin spalls and a completely rejuvenated simple burin. Only two flakes were unearthed, one of them a large flake made from a killiaq-like material.

Eigil Knuth related the narrow arrowhead to the Denbigh Culture. Thus he perceived this artefact, together with some artefacts from other ruins (e.g. the large adze preform made from dolerite in A2) as evidence of fast migration from Alaska to Greenland. The absolute dating of marine bone from ruins F6, A2 and C3 could support his theory. However, the stemmed end blades in ruin F7 did not 'fit' with the Denbigh artefact types and its presence confused his impression of a Denbigh relation.

A modern re-examination of the ruin F7 inventory considers the stemmed end blades in combination with simple burins, arrowheads and narrow micro blades as a typical Pre-Dorset inventory. This conclusion also explains why Knuth had so many difficulties in determining who made the ruin F7 inventory: For the first time in Arctic archaeology a High Arctic Pre-Dorset site was excavated, and naturally it showed a different typology and technology from what Knuth had experienced and excavated before.

Ruin area F
Ruin F7

Burins	1
Burin spalls	2
Stemmed end blades	2
Arrowhead	1
Micro blades	1
Flakes	2
Total	9

Ruin F8

This ruin was only partly visible on the terrace (figure 2.56). It was placed at the edge of the plateau, 4–5 metres south of a line between ruin F7 and F9. The ruin was never excavated and no finds are registered from it.

2.56 Ruin F8. The ruin was never excavated. Photo E. Knuth

Ruin F9

Artefact no. LI.7369–70, LI.10523–27

In the line of ruins F4, F6 and F7, approximately 16 m southeast of F7, ruin F9 is found. It was partly excavated in 1960 (figure 2.57) and re-excavated and drawn in 1990 (figures 2.58 & 2.59). It consists of a double periphery of oval shape, measuring 4.0 × 3.4 m. Ruin F9 thus reminded Eigil Knuth of ruin F7. A pavement across the ruin made Knuth believe that it had a mid-passage construction. However, the excavation convinced him that the central pavement actually had been circular and that it contained a fireplace. Another fireplace with layers of ashes was located south of the central fireplace inside the ruin.

THE ARCHAEOLOGY OF OLD NUULLIIT

2.57 Ruin F9 during excavation in 1990. Photo E. Knuth

2.58
A fireplace uncovered in ruin F9, in 1990. Photo E. Knuth

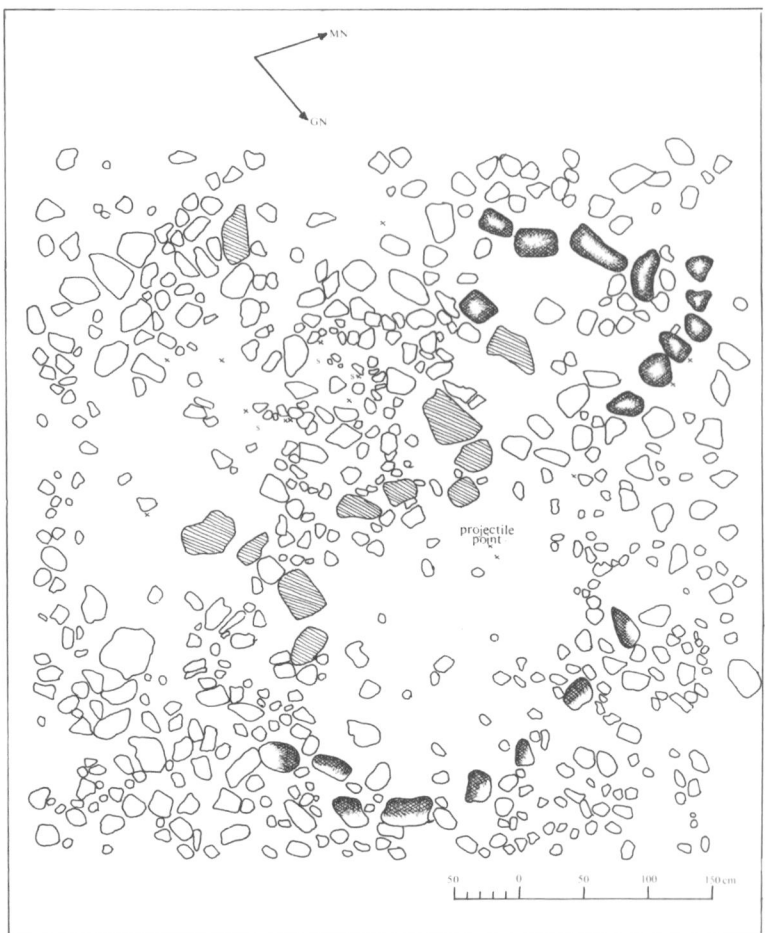

2.59
Plan of ruin F9.
Drawing
T. Grønnegaard

Inventory, technology and tradition: ruin F9 (figure 2.60)
Inventory from this ruin was recovered during two field-seasons (1960 and 1990). The only formal tool type is a distal end of a relatively large bifacial knife type, but since the base is absent it cannot be determined as to which tradition it belongs.

Ruin area F
Ruin F9

Burin spalls	4
Other biface/fragments	1
Flakes	22
Total	27

Four burin spalls were found placing the inventory in an early Palaeo-Eskimo context. The flakes (22 pieces) are from a bifacial production.

2.60 Inventory from ruin F9. Photo J. Sørensen

Ruin F10
This ruin is the most southern ruin at the F-plateau. It is situated 5 m southeast of ruin F9, and in its appearance it is like ruin F9 (figure 2.61). The ruin was excavated during 1960 (figure 2.61) and drawn in 1990 (figure 2.62). No finds derive from the ruin.

2.61
Ruin F10.
Photo E. Knuth

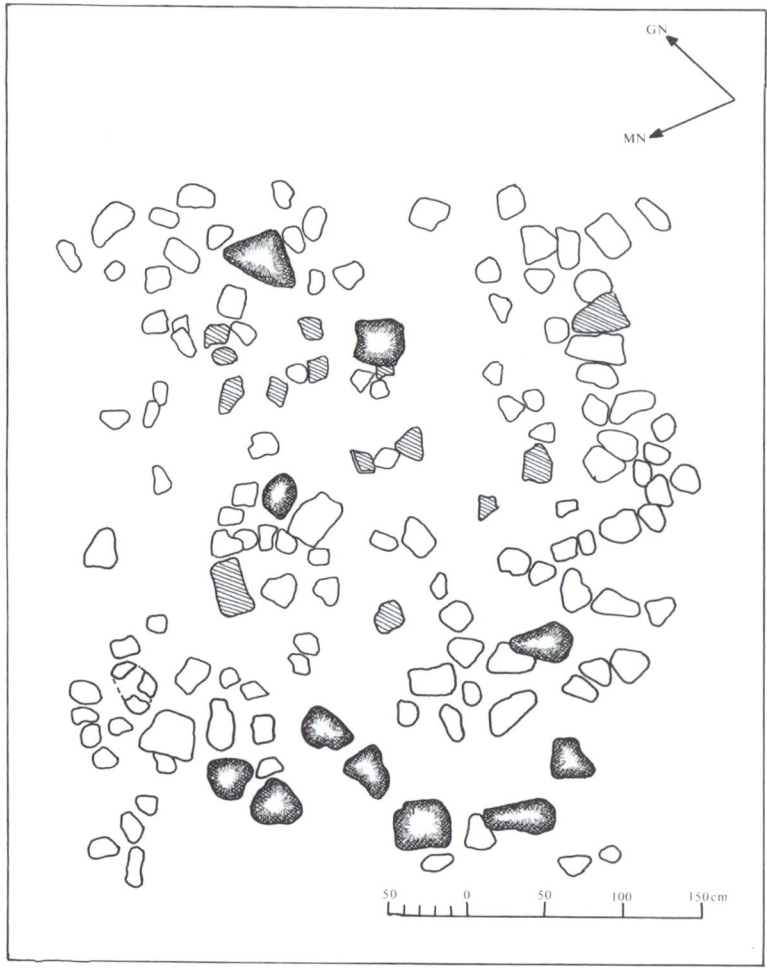

2.62
Plan of ruin F10.
Drawing
T. Grønnegaard

Ruin F11
Ruin F11 was earlier registered as 'tomt 14'. It is a large nearly invisible tent ring, placed at the edge of the F-plateau with its front against the shoreline. It is situated 10–15 m southwest of ruin F5. The ruin was not excavated and no finds derive from this ruin.

Ruin F12
Ruin F12 was earlier registered as 'tomt 16'. It is an almost invisible tent ring, placed at the edge of the F-plateau, against the sea. The ruin is situated approximately 6 m southeast of ruin F11. The ruin was not excavated and no finds derive from this ruin.

Ruin without number
Situated just short of a dozen metres SW of ruins F2 and F3, and just east of the above mentioned large boulder favoured by birds. The ruin lay so deep in the rocky landscape that it did not easily lend itself to recognition.

Conclusions on technology and tradition at the F-plateau
Based on technology and typology, the ruins F4 and F7 can be determined as formerly occupied by Palaeo-Eskimos from the Pre-Dorset tradition. Ruins F3, F6, F9 can all be attributed to an early Palaeo-Eskimo occupation. However, Saqqaq can be ruled out due to their raw material choice and the burin technology, thus either Independence I or Pre-Dorset people must have produced the ruins. Yet it should be remarked that neither the production of broad micro blades nor the production of flake blanks from tabular cores by indirect technique, both typical technologies of Independence I, are present in the inventory at the F-plateau. It is therefore suggested that the ruins at the F-plateau generally are remnants from a fairly large Canadian Pre-Dorset occupation.

2.1.8 The H-plateau

The structures at the H-plateau are generally different and often more solidly built than at higher plateaus (figure 2.63). Eigil Knuth found the structures already during his first season at Nuulliit in 1958. He considered them, from the beginning, as belonging to the Palaeo-Eskimo period, one of the reasons being that he managed to surface collect a large bifacial lithic knife and a lithic harpoon end blade at the H-plateau. However, he soon discovered that the structures were not typical Palaeo-Eskimo architecture and he therefore in some contexts operated with the term 'Meso-Eskimo site'. In Knuth's publication about Nuulliit (1977/78), he also refers to these structures as: 'Shelter ruins (Dorset ?)'. Knuth's own descriptions justify (see below) that the structures at this plateau must generally be considered as small solidly built tent rings or shelters belonging to the Thule Culture.

Eigil Knuth excavated several of the structures but he was never able to find an inventory inside any of the structures. In his later manuscript he does not conclude anything about their cultural attribution. However, he refers to them as 'shelter ruins', which we today acknowledge as a ruin type comprising structures such as small tent houses and hunter's beds, belonging to the Thule culture. It therefore seems most possible that the structures at the H-plateau generally belong to the Thule Culture, but that the plateau also was used by Late Dorset Palaeo-Eskimos. However, we cannot rule out that some of the houses or structures at this plateau have been made and used by the Late Dorset people.

2.63 The H-plateau with ruins. Photo E. Knuth

In the following description, the structures at this plateau are referred to as 'houses' due to their solidly built nature compared to the other ruins at Nuulliit.

Twelve structures in total are registered at the H-plateau lying side by side, approximately 50 m in front of the F-plateau, and 40 m from the sea. This plateau is 8.50 m above the present sea level. None of the structures of this type has a higher location than this. A fireplace was found at the slope in front of the plateau towards the sea, 7.75–8.00 m above sea level. This slope has vegetation consisting of grass and dryas. Half way down the slope, approximately 20 m from the sea, a 1½ m high wall, made by erosion from the sea, appears. The sea does not reach this wall today, not even at high tide.

The houses are different concerning morphology and preservation. However, because they were situated close to each other, Knuth perceived them as belonging to the same cultural period. Rudimentary structures, hard to distinguish from the gravel surface itself also appear. Knuth interpreted these as short-term used tent foundations from summer occupations.

From north-west to south-east the ruins are:

Houses 1, 2 and 3
These consist of three nearly invisible stone pavements lying around a stony elevation. In House 1 weak traces of a central fireplace appeared. In front of House 2 a group of large boulders were placed, probably a cache. No artefacts were found. House 3 was not described.

House 4
House 4 was found 13 paces east of House 3, hidden in the boulder field. No artefacts were found here.

House 5
This house was also registered as ruin H2 (figures 2.64 & 2.65). Two metres behind House 4 a stone circle, 1 m in diameter, was found. Between House 4 and 5 a bifacial knife made from green mcq was found (artefact no. LI.7371).

Ruin area H
House H5

Stemmed end blades	1
Flakes	1
Total	2

2.64
House 5 (H2) after excavation. Photo E. Knuth

2.65
Plan of House 5 (H2). Drawing T. Grønnegaard

House 6
This structure is situated eight paces east of House 4. It was solidly built and easy to recognize on the plateau. The vegetation was removed inside the periphery on 25 August 1958.

The ground plan of the house was trapezoidal but with rounded corners. Large stones placed side by side, with their flat sides facing inside, made up the periphery. In the front wall an 88 cm broad entrance was seen. The walls were up to 30 cm high. The back wall was straight, but the side walls were convex, leaving spaces for niches inside the house. Outside the periphery several rows of stones were placed, and Knuth interprets these as stones for holding the tent. Thus he considers the solid periphery as an inner panel.

The removal of the vegetation, primarily dryas, revealed a sterile sandy floor and some larger stones. A 60 cm large flagstone was found on the floor, but there was no construction of a platform front edge. Nevertheless, Knuth supposes that the back of the house served as a sleeping platform. In front of the entrance, on each side, two rows of stones were placed, as though there had been a small entrance to the house. To the right side of this entrance construction a fireplace built from stones was found, but neither ashes nor charcoal were found inside. No artefacts were found inside or around the house.

House 7
A small stone circle with a nearly invisible stone pavement was found behind House 6.

House 8
A nearly invisible house was found eight paces east of House 6. Two groups of stones were found in front of the house.

House 9
This House was found seven paces east of House 8. It consisted of a solidly built foundation of trapezoidal ground plan (figure 2.66), similar to House 6. Only the back wall was undisturbed and consisted of five stones placed side by side. Even though some of the front wall was eroded and had fallen over the edge of the plateau, a 65 cm broad entrance was discovered.

The distance from the front wall to the back wall was 3.5 m. And the maximum width of the house was 2.5 m. A circle of stones in front of the front wall could be perceived as a fireplace, but no ash or charcoal was found in it. No artefacts or bone materials were found in connection with House 9.

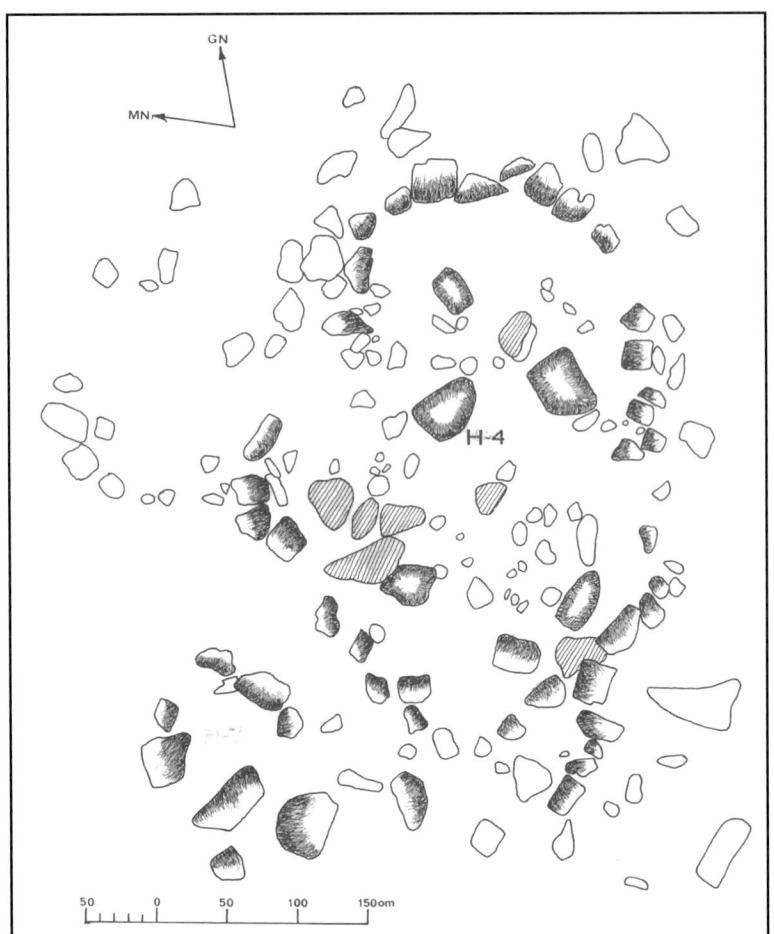

2.66
Plan of House 9 (H4). Drawing T. Grønnegaard

House 10
Close behind House 9's north-eastern corner, a convex row of small stones marked that House 9 was placed partially on top of an older house with the same kind of ground plan. In the middle of the older house, termed House 10, an ash pit was found.

House 11
Four metres behind House 9 a circle of stones was found, lying nearly invisible deep in the gravel. On the edge of the plateau, in front of House 10 and 11, two groups of large stones were placed. Probably they were former meat caches. At the slope in front of Houses 9, 10 and 11, two fireplaces were found. None of them contained pieces of charcoal large enough for a conventional ^{14}C-dating.

House 12

House 12 was also termed ruin H5. This house was situated at nine paces east of House 9. It was excavated during the 1958 season and drawn in 1990 (figure 2.67). The ground plan is described precisely as that of House 6. It had a stone-built wall foundation and an outside lying periphery of smaller stones. The distance from the front wall to the back wall was 2.0 m. The side walls were convex. The maximum width of the house was 2.3 m. The entrance was situated in the front wall a little to the west of its centre.

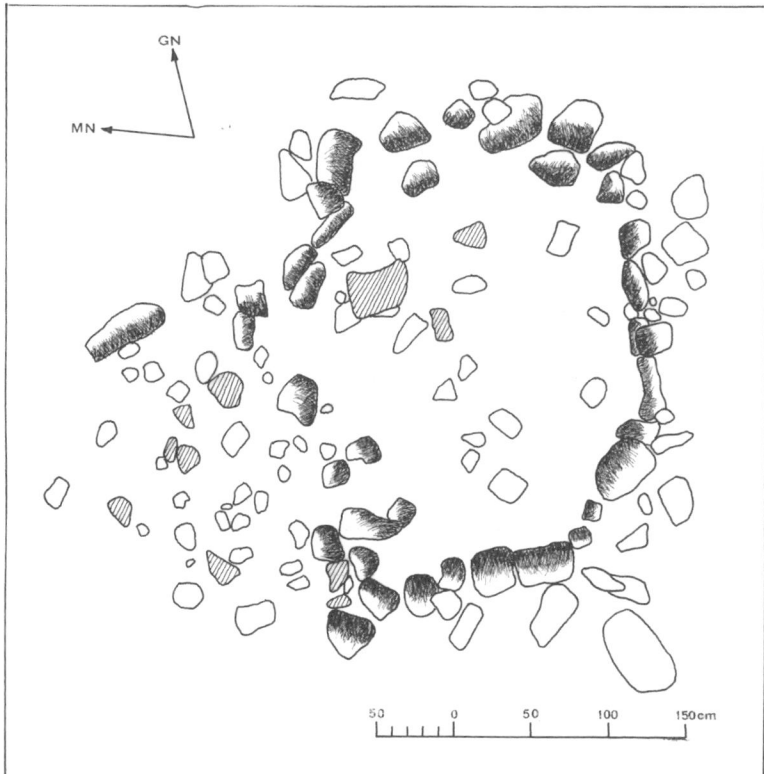

2.67
Plan of House 12 (H5). Drawing T. Grønnegaard

After removing the vegetation, mainly dryas, and excavating the floor, Eigil Knuth found two circular-like pavements, but no charcoal or ashes were found in association. However, 0.75 m in front of the entrance a fireplace with layers of ashes was located. On the surface of this fireplace, Knuth found a triangular lithic harpoon head with a concave base (no. LI.7372) and further down the slope two small flakes were collected (LI.9981).

THE ARCHAEOLOGY OF OLD NUULLIIT

Lithic inventory found at the H-plateau (figures 2.68, 2.69 & 2.70)
Between House 5 and House 4 a large bifacial stemmed end blade with a broken distal end was found. The end blade must be considered as a typical Dorset knife type. The end blade is, as the only tool at Nuulliit, made from a fine-grained strong green, slightly translucent mcq. This type of raw material most probably comes from an outcrop in Rensselaer Bay, northern Thule region (Sørensen 2006a: 39). It thus seems most likely that Late Dorset people, coming from the northern Thule region, brought it to Nuulliit. A single flake was also picked up in this area.

2.68
Artefacts found at the H-plateau near House 5 (H2). Photo J. Sørensen

2.69
Artefacts found at the H-plateau near House 12 (H5). Photo J. Sørensen

In a fireplace in front of House 12, a harpoon end blade with a strong concave base was found. The harpoon end blade is perfectly shaped by pressure retouch and is made from grey-white mcq. It has a broken basal corner. This type of harpoon end blade is typical of the Late Dorset Palaeo-Eskimo tradition.

Only three lithic artefacts were discovered from the H-plateau despite Eigil Knuth's persistent surveys and excavations. Moreover, none of the lithics were found inside the ruins. Generally the ruins at this plateau must be regarded as small tent houses and hunter's beds of 'shelter type' made by the Thule Culture, while the lithics are typical of the Late Dorset.

From re-studying artefacts and structures at the H-plateau it must be concluded that both Late Dorset people and Thule Inuit used this area. The Thule Inuit left their small but solidly built tent-house structures behind, while the Late Dorset people so far are documented only by a few lithic artefacts.

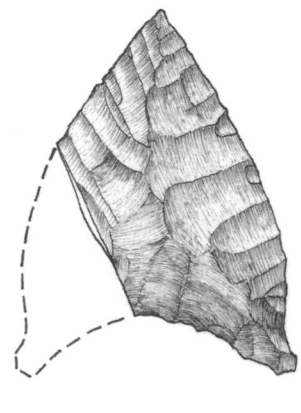

2.70 Lithic tool types found at the H-plateau. Drawing H.C. Gulløv

Ruin area H
House H12

Harpoon end blade	1
Flakes	2
Bone material	1
Total	4

2.1.9 The I-area

The houses in this area lie at different elevations on a rock, about 100 m southeast of the H-plateau, separated from the H-plateau by a lowering in the landscape. The house ruins cannot be culturally and chronologically attributed to any specific tradition or culture, but at least House 1 seems to be of a similar type as the trapezoidal house structures at the H-plateau from the Thule Culture.

House 1

This is the northernmost situated house at the I-area. It is placed on an isolated rock shelf approximately 9.0–9.5 m above sea level. The house has a well-preserved wall construction made from stones placed side by side. The ground plan is trapezoidal. It measures 2.7 × 2.2 m. The floor consists of gravel in which dryas and grey lichens grow. No artefacts were found in relation to this house.

Houses 2, 3 and 4

Three oval formations made from stones were lying a few metres lower than House 1, towards the south and the seashore. The houses were built up against a large rock. All the ovals were built from closely placed stones. Three large flagstones, lying in a row, separated the floor into two in House 4. Eigil Knuth had seen this phenomenon before, in Peary Land. This oval measured approximately 150 × 100 cm. House 1 contained a drill bit of slate with a ground wide and flat shank and a slender working point. House 3 contained a fragmentary piece of ground slate. Thus the three stone oval constructions should be regarded as belonging to the Thule Culture.

House 5

Much lower than the other houses in this area, at about 4 m above sea level, House 5 was found. This house was lying by the sea-eroded wall. Three or four stone constructions outside the house had fallen into the sea. These could have been parts of former caches.

2.2 Organic material from Old Nuulliit

The organic preservation at Nuulliit is unfortunately bad and only a few organic artefacts were therefore found. No middens or permafrozen layers with artefacts have been found in relation to any of the ruins from Old Nuulliit. Moreover, the subsoil at the Nuulliit peninsula is probably slightly acidic due to the volcanic basalts (dolerite) and the lack of chalk/lime deposits in the local geology. From New Nuulliit permafrozen midden layers in Thule Inuit turf-built winter houses have produced a varied and comprehensive organic artefact material (Holtved 1954).

From Old Nuulliit the following organic materials or artefacts were found (see table 1).

Ruin no.	No.	Material	Stored at	Comment
A2	(L1.9983)	Piece of walrus tusk	The Danish National Museum	Used for radiocarbon analysis (K-2561)
A2	(L1.9984)	Unidentified piece of bone. Probably a badly preserved pressure point	The Danish National Museum	
A2	(L1.9985)	Unidentified bone with joint partly preserved	The Danish National Museum	
C3	(L1.9986) (L1.9987)	Bone from polar bear identified as humerus	The Danish National Museum	Used for radiocarbon analysis (K-2560)
F4	(L1.7357)	Worked whalebone, (possible fragment of a sledge shoe)	The Danish National Museum	
F6	(L1.7359)	Pieces of whalebone, (possible fragment of a sledge shoe)	The Danish National Museum	Used for radiocarbon analysis (K-1628)
H4	(L1.7376)	Unidentified small pieces of burnt bone	The Danish National Museum	
H5	(L1.7375)	Piece of walrus tusk. Probably a former worked artefact	The Danish National Museum	
K1	(L1.7377)	Unidentified piece of bone	The Danish National Museum	

Table 1.
Organic material found at Old Nuulliit

Not much can be concluded on the basis of the organic material found at Old Nuulliit due to its low representativity. It is interesting to note that the marine mammals dominate the bone material. It indicates that marine mammals were the prime game for people living at Nuulliit. The pieces of walrus tusk suggest that the early Palaeo-Eskimos hunted these large animals, maybe even here from Nuulliit. A single bone of polar bear suggests that bears were hunted too already by the Independence I Palaeo-Eskimos.

2.3 Absolute dating

Six radiocarbon datings have been made of material from Old Nuulliit. The first five are conventional datings made at the laboratory in Copenhagen. The last dating is an AMS dating made by the laboratory in Kiel. Eigil Knuth had three datings made during the 1970s on marine bone or tusk material. The three dates must be considered unreliable in an archaeological context due to the marine reservoir effect (marine species intake of old ^{14}C) (Dumond and Griffin 2002). The high ^{13}C value of the analysed bone samples indicates that the bones must be younger than their radiocarbon age and the dating can as such be used as evidence for a maximum age of the material. In relation to McCullough and Schledermann's survey in North Greenland and at Old Nuulliit, two more datings were made from Nuulliit (K-6063, K-6064). One of a walrus bone from ruin F7 (K-6064), a dating that can only be used as a maximum age. However, this dating produced a quite late date (1970–1740 BC) despite its high ^{13}C value, and thereby indicates that ruin F7 does not belong to a first migration into Greenland. The second dating (K-6063) was made on a matrix of charcoal from a hearth row. The species of the burnt wood was not determined before the dating and we can therefore not for certain exclude that drift wood with a high own age was part of the sample. However, if the charcoal consisted of local wood we must consider this dating as only slightly older than the hearth row. The last dating (KIA-32917) was run in relation to the present re-analysis and publication of Nuulliit. The dated material consisted of charcoal from ruin C1 and determined by specialist C. Malmros, at the National Museum of Denmark, to be of the local grown species (*Salix arctica*). The dating should thus be correct in relation to use of the fireplace, although the willow could have some own age before it was burnt.

To conclude, it can be stated that the radiocarbon datings made from Old Nuulliit, except the last one from ruin C1, generally do not stand up to a modern archaeological standard, and that they therefore only can be used as indications of maximum ages. Ruin C1 came out with a dating indicating that this ruin was in use in the 20th century BC, corresponding to the late Independence I phase. The maximum age of ruin F7 to the 19th Century BC is not as old as expected by Eigil Knuth. Thus one important result from a critical review of the ^{14}C-dating is that neither of the ^{14}C-datings can document a particular early settlement phase at Nuulliit, in contrast to what was expected and believed by Knuth.

Site	Lab.no.	Year	Material	Cultural attribution	¹³C	¹⁴C Bp (uncal)	¹⁴C BC cal (one sigma)*	Excavator	Reference
Nuulliit, hearth row	K-6063	1993	Matrix of charcoal	Late Dorset	-22.4	1340+/-55	640–770 AD	P. Schledermann	(Schledermann and McCullough 1992)
Nuulliit, ruin F7	K-6064	1993	Walrus bone	Pre-Dorset	-15.1	3530+/-85	1970–1740	E. Knuth	File no. NMVIII 4849, Danish National Museum
Nuulliit, Ruin C3	K-2560	1976	Polar bear bone	Independence I	-12.4	5060+/-95	3970–3760	E. Knuth	File no. NMVIII 4849, Danish National Museum
Nuulliit, Ruin A2	K-2561	1976	Walrus tusk	Independence I	-13.2	3770+/-50	2290–2060	E. Knuth	File no. NMVIII 4849, Danish National Museum
Nuulliit Ruin F6	K-1628	1970	Whale bone	Pre-Dorset	-	4500+/-110	3360–3020	E. Knuth	File n. NMVIII 4849, Danish National Museum
Nuulliit Ruin C1	KIA-32917	2007	Charcoal (Salix arctica)	Independence I	-26.3	3675+/-40	2135-1979	E. Knuth, T. Grønnegaard C.K. Jensen	

(* calibrated by Oxcal, version 3.10.0.1)

Table 2.

Radiocarbon dating analysis made from Old Nuulliit

2.4 Later archaeological investigations at Nuulliit

Two years after Eigil Knuth's last season at Nuulliit the Canadian archaeologists P. Schledermann and K. McCullough visited and surveyed Nuulliit during a few days (Schledermann and McCullough 1992). The stay at Nuulliit was not planned but forced due to a shipwreck off Nuulliit. During their stay they found a hearth row on the Nuulliit peninsula. It was 11 m long and consisted of seven hearth units. Moreover, single hearths were located in a parallel line about 1.5 m east of this main row. A radiocarbon date was made on mixed charcoal from one of the single hearths calibrated to AD 640–770 (K-6063). The find and the dating document a type of Late Dorset structure that is known from Ellesmere Island (Schledermann 1990) and the northern Thule area in Hatherton Bay (Appelt and Gulløv 1999). This kind of structure is currently interpreted as a communal structure and it indicates aggregation of many Late Dorset people (seven families?) at certain seasons at Nuulliit (Appelt 2003). The hearth row is so far the most southern communal structure from Late Dorset in Greenland and it adds one more aspect to Nuulliit's status as an important prehistoric site.

3.0 Discussion

3.1 The settlements at Old Nuulliit and their cultural affiliations

Due to Eigil Knuth's excavations and a technological and typological analysis of the lithic material we can conclude that the first people who came to Nuulliit belonged to the Independence I Palaeo-Eskimo tradition. We know that the Independence I tradition appeared in the High Arctic approximately between 2500–1900 BC (Grønnow and Jensen 2003) and that the Independence I ruin C1 at Nuulliit was in use in the late Independence I phase (probably in the 20th century BC). The ruins that belong to the Independence I tradition lie in four groups, within an area of a diameter of 300 m. Typically the ruins are situated on small promontories, raised beaches, between 9–11 m above present sea level. In total the Independence I settlement consists of nine tent rings and two caches. The four Independence dwelling groups are termed A, C, D, and E.

Group A consists of two ruins both fairly rich in lithic artefacts (151 and 240 pieces). The tools and production processes reflected in the material suggest that a great variety of tasks were carried out at the A-plateau: blades have been produced, bifaces for weapons have been repaired and produced, skins have been scraped and tools made from organic materials have been shaped by use of burins.

The architecture of the A ruins are circular and rather large, up to 4–5 m in diameter. This type of ruin would be typical of a tent construction. Ruin A1 and A2 are well built with several stones in the periphery and maybe double peripheries. Possibly large stones were used for anchoring the tent constructions. The reason for the solid construction of the tent ruins was probably the very windy conditions at Nuulliit that Eigil Knuth also experienced. Outside ruin A1 an activity area including a scraper and some micro blades were found. This area suggests that someone, maybe a woman, has been working outside the tent, but it also suggests that the tent probably was in use during the summer when it was possible to work outside. The amount of lithic material and the range of the tools suggest that the ruins at the A-plateau have been occupied once, probably within some weeks, during a summer in the Independence I period.

Very much the same pattern as at the A-plateau is observed at the plateaus C and D. Ruins at the C-plateau comprise of three circular or slightly oval tent rings and two caches. The tent rings resemble ruins at plateau A. However, there is evidence of a centrally built fireplace in ruin C1, constructed from many small stone slabs. In ruins C2 and C3 some flagstones are situated centrally and these could well be part of the mid-passage floor division that is often seen in the Independence I architecture. Due to the amount of the lithics (C1: 126 pieces, C2: 46 pieces, C3: 145 pieces) and the low variety of tools found in the tent rings, it is possible that the three tent rings were only used during one stay. However, the two well-built caches suggest, if they belong to this occupation, that a good hunting bag was stored here for future use, and that people therefore could have used these dwellings during later visits.

There are two circular tent rings at the D-plateau. Both show an uncharacteristic layout with several flagstones inside. When analysing the artefacts found in ruin D1, it was seen that this ruin had a very high ratio of lithic debitage in relation to tools and preforms. The persons who used dwelling D1 obviously came with a good supply of lithic raw material and exploited it here. However, they also brought the tools with them. The large amount of lithics found in ruin D1 does as such not necessarily reflect a long stay; rather, it represents a specific process. In ruin D2 only three pieces of lithics were found, which could indicate that this dwelling was used only briefly.

Plateau E yielded two tent rings, but only ruin E2 was investigated by Eigil Knuth. This ruin is smaller, only 2 m in diameter, than the other Independence I ruins, and its location on the edge of an area with dolerite columns far from the sea and high in the terrain is atypical. In the ruin only a single burin spall was found together with 404 pieces of debris. We might therefore imagine that this small structure was hastily set up and used by a person who processed some tools during a short stay. The location close to the dolerite columns could indicate that the person or persons needed shelter from a specific wind direction. However, the reason for ruin E2's atypical appearance and location could also be explained by the fact that it was used during another season than the other dwellings. It is not certain if the second ruin at the E-plateau was used at the same time, but its close lying position makes it most probable.

The F-plateau
South of the A-, C-, D- and E-plateaus on which ruins from the Independence I tradition were situated, a fifth Palaeo-Eskimo ruin group was found on the F-plateau. On this long and narrow plateau, twelve ruins are placed as pearls on a string within a distance of approximately 100 m. All twelve ruins are interpreted as tent rings, but only five of them (F3, F4, F6, F7, F9) were excavated or partly excavated. From two other ruins (F1, F2) surface collections are present.

DISCUSSION

When analysing the lithic technology from a dynamical technological perspective we realize that some of the tent rings includes lithics processed in a different technology than at the other ruins and plateaus at Nuulliit. Plateau F also shows formal tool types that generally are not found in the Independence I culture. The blade production is limited at the F-plateau, and the blades are narrow and thin compared to the Independence I blades, while still of high regularity and quality. The production of burins and burin spalls are more accurate and include thinner burin spalls than in the inventory from the Independence I ruins. Two stemmed end blades of morphology typical to Pre-Dorset and Greenlandic Dorset appear in ruin F7. However, they appear in combination with arrowheads and true burins, as they were produced during the Early Palaeo-Eskimo period. This combination of artefacts has not appeared in Greenland before and we therefore must compare with material from the Canadian Arctic to understand who made them. The closest material, which reflects this kind of inventory and tradition, is found in a Palaeo-Eskimo ruin termed 'Feature 2' from Ridge Site, Ellesmere Island (Schledermann 1990: 122). Feature 2 has, in its inventory, the same kind of stemmed end blades in combination with burins and slender micro blades as seen in ruin F7. Feature 2, and Ridge Site in general, is attributed to the Canadian Pre-Dorset. For these reasons it must be concluded that ruin F7 was used by people of the Pre-Dorset tradition.

From ruin F4 at Nuulliit more signs of Pre-Dorset lithic technology are observed. First of all we see a burin re-sharpened from the burin edge by a series of small flakes. This method is diagnostic of Pre-Dorset technology and is only recorded one time before in Greenland, at ruin 13 at Solbakken, Hall land, as an indication of Pre-Dorset here (Grønnow and Sørensen 2006; Sørensen 2006a, Sørensen 2011).

The conclusion is that the ruins, which can be related to a Palaeo-Eskimo tradition at the F-plateau, must be related to the Pre-Dorset tradition.

The architecture of the ruins at the F-plateau seems to be homogeneous. Generally the structures are round to slightly oval tent rings of 3–5 m in diameter, built from stones often with slabs in the middle indicating central features and sometimes fireplaces. Some of the tent rings have a double periphery, and in some situations large naturally situated stones could have been used as 'anchors' in the construction. Thus the double periphery and the use of anchoring stones seem to be seen in several of the ruin groups as a characteristic of Nuulliit, rather than a culturally dependent kind of architecture.

The short distance between the tents at the F-plateau, and the fact that the inventories can be technologically and typologically attributed to the Pre-Dorset tradition, suggest that this ruin group was used simultaneously by one large group of people, e.g. 10 families. Thus for the first time a group of Pre-Dorset Palaeo-

Eskimos is archaeologically described in Greenland. The information that groups of Pre-Dorset Palaeo-Eskimos travelled around in the Thule region adds a new dimension to our understanding of the prehistory of Greenland, and especially to the complexity of the cultural history of the Thule region. How far did the Pre-Dorset penetrate into Greenland and did they meet people from the Independence or Saqqaq tradition in North Greenland?

Dating the ruins at the F-plateau
One dating from a walrus bone in ruin F7 provided a date calibrated to 1970–1740 BC. Knowing that this date cannot be trusted due to the marine reservoir effect ($^{13}C = -15.3$), it still suggests that the Pre-Dorset occupation at Nuulliit did not happen before this time, but after.

At Ridge Site, on Knud Peninsula, Elllesmere Island, the ruin 'feature 2' which, judged from its inventory and technology could be contemporaneous with Nuulliit ruin F7, was excavated (Schledermann 1990: 93). Two dates were produced from feature 2 (TO 1638 and GSC2827) on respectively charcoal of willow (*Salix arctica*) from a fireplace in feature 2, and unspecified bone (Schledermann 1990: 343). The date of the unspecified bone material has to be rejected as it is most possible a bone from a marine mammal. The dating of the willow charcoal produced the date 3440 +/-50 uncal. BP calibrated to 1880–1680 BC. Thus it seems probable that the occupation of the Pre-Dorset ruin 7 at the F-plateau happened around 1800–1600 BC.

The ruins at the plateaus B, H and I represent structures mainly of shelter type, i.e. small solidly built tent houses and hunters' beds from the Thule Culture. Eigil Knuth invested much energy in investigating these structures, as he believed that they represented a 'third' Independence culture in North Greenland. Generally he was not able to attribute any artefacts to these structures even though he tried hard. If some of these structures had been made and used by Palaeo-Eskimos (despite their Thule architecture), one would expect that Knuth had found at least a few pieces of lithics inside them, but he never did. Nevertheless, at the H-plateau he surface collected some lithics *between* the structures, e.g. a large bifacial knife of Late Dorset type. These artefacts generally confused more than explained the situation to him. Probably the case is that both Thule and Late Dorset people used the H-plateau. The Thule people built the shelter ruins after Late Dorset had used the plateau.

The presence of winter houses and shelter ruins at Nuulliit indicates that the Thule people used the peninsula in different seasons. At the westernmost part of Nuulliit, 'New Nuulliit', the Inuit winter houses probably were used from September to April. When arriving at Nuulliit at other times of the year, in other situations and for shorter occupations, a different architecture and a different location

DISCUSSION

was sometimes chosen by the Thule Inuit. Seemingly, a more sheltered place lying higher in the terrain was often chosen for the shelter ruins. Also Holtved's Group III at New Nuulliit can be seen as such an example.

Moreover, the local conditions at Nuulliit have to be considered in relation to the architecture. The many small well-built shelter ruins from the Thule period, but also the many examples of double peripheries in the tent rings from the Palaeo-Eskimo period, might be an indication of an adjustment to the specific natural conditions. Probably wind and weather conditions at this barren, north-westernmost tip of Greenland have always been rough.

Ruin area	A	A	A	C			D		E	F							H		
Ruin	A1	A1b	A2	C1	C2	C3	D1	D2	E2	F1	F2	F3	F4	F6	F7	F9	H2	H4	H5
End scrapers		1	1																
Side scrapers		1											1						
Burin preforms																			
Burins			2				1	1				1	1		1				
Burin spalls	3	2	13	3	2	4	12		1				3		2	4			
Bifacial preforms	1	2																	
Harpoon end blade preform						1													
Harpoon end blade														1					1
Stemmed end blades															2		1		
Other bifaces/fragments																1			
Arrow head preform	1		1																
Arrow head				1	2										1				
Adze preform			1																
Micro blades	1	2	16	10	2	2	3	1					3		1				
Micro blade cores	2																		
Other cores																			
Retouched pieces/other preforms		2		1	3	2	2						1						
Flakes and debris	90	43	204	110	40	135	799	1	404	30	10	22	13	5	2	22	1		2
Bone material			3			1							1	1				ben-kul	1
Total of lithics	98	53	240	126	49		817	3	405	30	10	23	22	7	9	27	2		4

Table 3.
Complete list of artefacts from all ruins at Old Nuullit

DISCUSSION

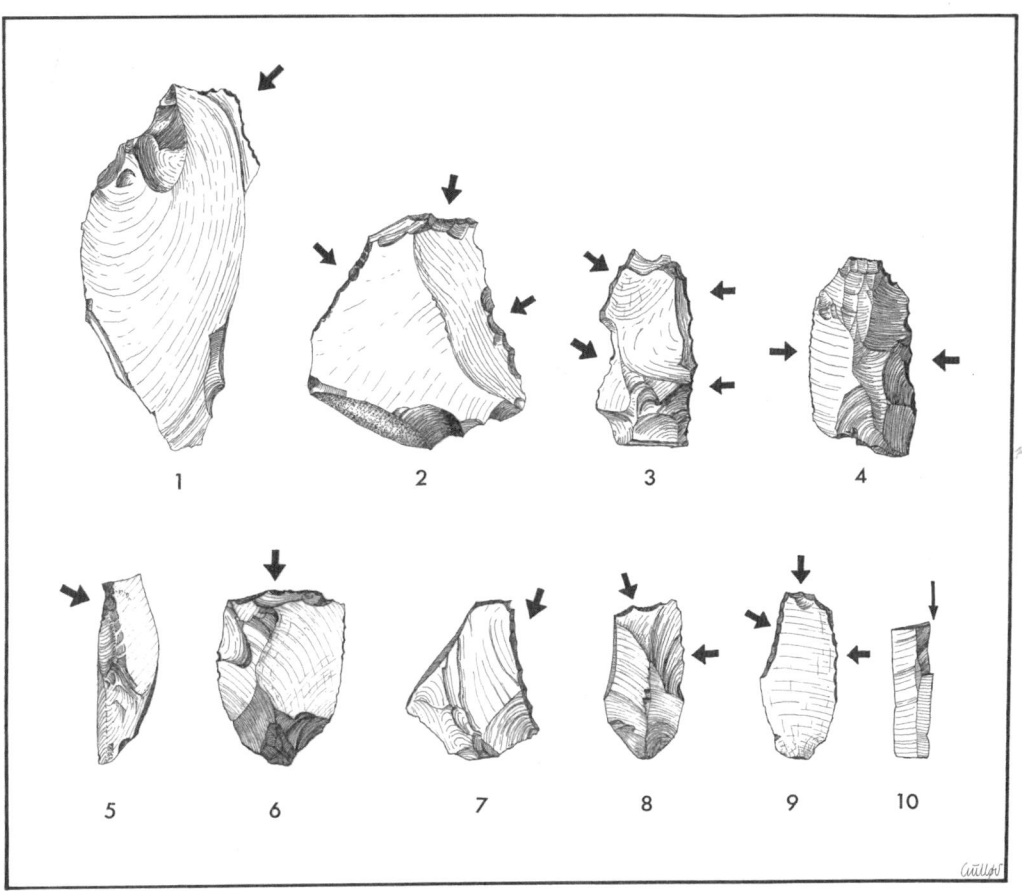

3.0 Lithic flakes with retouch interpret by Eigil as different tools.
Drawing H.C. Gulløv

DISCUSSION

3.2 Eigil Knuth as an archaeologist at Nuulliit

Eigil Knuth was generally very careful with registration and documentation at Nuulliit. Knuth and his assistants' (Claus Kjeld Jensen and Tim Grønnegaard) registrations, drawings and plans are detailed and of high quality. Knuth often excavated the ruins completely (inside) and he also mapped the distribution of the tools. However, due to weather conditions and logistics he did not always manage to complete every single ruin. Nevertheless, he managed, with the help of Jensen and Grønnegaard, during the 1990 season, to complete most of what he started during his four field campaigns. Photos, registration, drawings and diaries are ordered at the Knuth Archive at Queen's Library. Everything is numbered and catalogued including a description by Eigil Knuth, so it is certain from which ruin the pieces derive. The high standard of curation and documentation that Knuth maintained reflects the enormous respect he had for the material. Knut's archaeological investigations were an important part of his life and the artefacts from Nuulliit were among the most mysterious and precious to Knuth, probably because they, to him, represented an unsolved problem and therefore another potential adventure. For long periods he kept them in his private apartment, considering them his most precious treasure.

Eigil Knuth was an autodidact and a pioneer in archaeology (Grønnow and Jensen 2003). He relied upon only very few people when assessing the archaeological material. One of them was J.L. Giddings, who excavated at Cape Denbigh, another was B. Thostrup who participated in the 'Denmark Expedition' and pieced all the expeditions' archaeological observations together in a publication which Knuth respected highly.

In some respects Knuth linked up his archaeological conclusions on work from these two persons: Ruins and artefacts at plateau F were seen as related to the Denbigh tradition at Iyatayet, excavated by Giddings (Giddings 1964), while shelter ruins at Nuulliit were seen as being culturally connected to shelter ruins originally described by Bendix Thostrup in Northeast Greenland (Thostrup 1911).

Eigil Knuth had a tendency to focus on single artefacts, or single structural or architectural elements, and subsequently to draw conclusions based on the interpretation of these, rather than from complex contexts. In this way, two artefacts that were morphologically alike in two different regions could in Knuth's view amount to 'evidence', and be interpreted as having been made by the same people. However, such interpretations often led to contradictions, which often prevented Knuth to draw final conclusions and finish manuscripts.

3.3 Conclusions

Many new conclusions can be deduced from the reinvestigation of the archaeological material from Old Nuulliit. Some of the most important are:

Old Nuulliit was inhabited by the Independence I tradition. Tent rings related to this tradition are found at plateaus A, C, D and E, representing at least four different occupations, probably equivalent to four episodes.

A group of Canadian Pre-Dorset Palaeo-Eskimos settled at the F-plateau (at least 12 tent rings). It is the first time a site/group of the Pre-Dorset tradition is located archaeologically in Greenland.

All settlements and ruins seem, based on analyses of their artefact inventory and architecture, to have been used during single occupations. Thus each plateau probably represents single site occupations. Many of these ruins seem to have been in use for a short period of time, e.g. few weeks, due to their small lithic inventory, while other ruins have more numerous inventories. Thus these ruins could have been used for a longer period, e.g. during the winter.

Both Palaeo-Eskimo and Thule Inuit ruins are solidly built, with reinforcing elements, such as double peripheries and natural anchoring stones. The ruins at Old Nuulliit thus add variations to the prehistoric eastern Arctic architecture. The variations can probably be explained as local adjustments to the conditions at Nuulliit, and the variations thereby challenge our understanding of the Arctic 'ruin typology'.

4.0 Perspectives and potentials: Nuulliit and the archaeology of the Thule region

The Old Nuulliit site and its new interpretation add substantial knowledge to our understanding of the early prehistory in Greenland. Old Nuulliit is now the southern border of Independence I and Pre-Dorset in North Greenland. South of Nuulliit so far only the Saqqaq tradition and the Greenlandic Dorset tradition are found. The same can be concluded concerning the Late Dorset ceremonial aggregation sites, which in Greenland have not been found yet south of Nuulliit. An important perspective concerning the prehistory of Greenland is that the Thule area including Nuulliit seems to mark a shed between two culturally very different areas in Greenland: 1) the High Arctic Thule area connected via the North Water polynya to High Arctic Canada, Ellesmere Island and 2) the rest of Arctic and sub-Arctic Greenland. These two areas are each characterized by different occupations of people and cultural traditions from the first migrations in 2500 BC. The Thule area comprising the Nuulliit site seems to be a much more dynamic and culturally complex area than other regions of Greenland. So, too, does the cultural complexity at Nuulliit, through millennia, illustrate how the Thule area is a part of Canadian cultural history rather than Greenlandic cultural history. Thus, at certain times the Thule area seems to act as a filter in Greenland: so far there is no archaeological evidence that Pre-Dorset and Late Dorset migrated from the Thule area into Greenland.

Potentials and possible future research at Nuulliit
The archaeological investigations at Nuulliit have so far revealed evidence of Independence I, Pre-Dorset, Late Dorset and the Thule Culture. Only one stray find in Eigil Knuth's collection from Nuulliit indicates presence of Greenlandic Dorset: a micro blade made from transparent quartz crystal, with a retouched proximal end (a tang). Thus, ruins from the Greenlandic Dorset should be found somewhere in the Nuulliit area. Moreover, it is possible that people from the Saqqaq tradition have visited the site as well – since sites of this tradition are found both north and south of Nuulliit (Grønnow and Sørensen 2006).

The hearth row and the few Late Dorset artefacts raise the question about where the Late Dorset people also had their houses or tents at Nuulliit as it is the case in

Inglefield Land (Appelt et al. 1999). So far they have not been found. A future survey at Nuulliit could possibly locate Late Dorset house ruins.

Another interesting topic to study is the cultural relation between Late Dorset and early Thule during the 13th century AD at Nuulliit. When considering the possible cultural history at Nuulliit in relation to what so far is found and reported, one can state that Nuulliit possesses an unexploited archaeological potential, and that much archaeological survey and excavation still can be done at Nuulliit.

Several ruins found at Nuulliit were not excavated by Eigil Knuth, thus it would be interesting to return to the F-plateau and excavate one of the assumed Pre-Dorset tent rings and thereby further document this tradition in High Arctic Greenland. Moreover, by AMS dating charcoal of local wood and terrestrial bone materials from ruin contexts, it will be possible to date and re-date several of the Palaeo-Eskimo ruins and finally establish an absolute chronology at Nuulliit.

Appendix

List of place names and terminology

Danish	Former Greenlandic spelling	New Greenlandic spelling	English
Etah	Îta	Iita	
Umanaq	Ùmánaq	Uummannaq	
	Narssârssuk	Narsarsuk	
Booth Sund			Booth Sound
Parker Snow Bay	Ivssuvigsûp pâva	Issuvissuup Paava	Parker Snow Bay
Wolstenholme Fjord	Ùmánap kangerdlua	Uummannap Kangerlua	
Wolstenholme Ø	Qeqertarsuaq	Qeqertarssuaq	
Steensby Land	none		
Inglefield Bredning	Kangerdlugssuaq	Kangerlussuaq	Inglefield Gulf
Hoppner Næs	Angmârsiorfik	Ammaarsiorfik	Hoppner Ness
Washington Land	none		
Baffin Bugt			none
Kane Bassin			Kane Basin
Hakluyt Ø	Agpârssuit	Appaarsuit	
Herbert Ø	Qeqertarssuaq	Qeqertarssuaq	
Kap Calhoun			Cape Calhoun
Melville Bugt	Qimugseriarssuaq	Qimusseriarsuaq	
Saunders Ø	Agpat	Appat	
	UvdleUlli		
Pituffik Glacier	Pâkitsup sermerssua	Paakitsup Sermersua	
Olrik Fjord	Kangerdluarssuk	Kangerluarsorujuk	
Barden Bugt			
Granville Fjord	Iterdlagssuaq	Iterlassuaq	
	Ivssuvigsôq	Issuvissooq	
Rensselaer Bugt			
Kap Parry	Kangârssugssuaq	Kangaarsussuaq	
Littleton Ø	Pikiuleq	Pikiuleq	
	Neqe	Neqi	
Other			
Flint	Angmâq	Ammaq	microcrystalline quarts (mcq)

Bibliography

Appelt, M. (2003). *De sidste palæoeskimoer. Nordvest Grønland i perioden 800–1300 e.v.t.* Nationalmuseet, Danmark, unpublished Ph.D. thesis, Institute of Archaeology, Moesgaard, Aarhus University. Aarhus.

Appelt, M. and H. C. Gulløv (eds.) (1999). *Late Dorset in High Arctic Greenland. Final report on the Gateway to Greenland project.* Copenhagen, Danish Polar Centre, publication no. 7.

Appelt, M., H. Kapel and M. Zimmermann (2001). 'Arkæologisk rekognoscering i Thule kommune sommeren 1998'. Internal report, The National Museum of Denmark, no. 62.

Bennike, O. and C. Andreasen (2005). 'Radiocarbon dating of musk-ox (Ovibos moschatus) remains from northeast Greenland'. *Polar Record* vol. 41, no. 219: 305–310.

Born, E. (2005). *Grønlands hvalrosser.* Nuuk, Ilinniusiorfik.

Dahl-Jensen, D., K. Mosegaard, N. Gundestrup, G.D Clow, S.J. Johnsen, A.W. Hansen and N. Balling (1998). 'Past Temperatures Directly from the Greenland Ice Sheet'. *Science* no. 82: 268–271.

Dawes, P. (2006). 'Explanatory notes to the Geological map of Greenland, 1:500 000, Thule, Sheet 5'. Copenhagen, GEUS.

Dumond, D. E. and D. G. Griffin (2002). 'Measurements on the Marine Reservoir Effect on Radiocarbon Ages in the Eastern Bering Sea'. *Arctic* (1): 77–86.

Giddings, J. L. (1964). *The Archaeology of Cape Denbigh.* Providence, Rhode Island, Brown University Press.

Gilberg, R. (1994). *Mennesket Minik (1888–1918) en grønlænders liv mellem 2 verdener.* Espergærde, ILBE.

Grønnow, B. and M. Sørensen (2006). 'Palaeo-Eskimo Migrations into Greenland: The Canadian Connection'. In: J. Arneborg and B. Grønnow (eds.), *Dynamics of Northern Societies. Proceedings from the Sila/Nabo conference, May 2004*. Copenhagen, Nationalmuseet, 59–74.

Grønnow, B. and J.F. Jensen (2003). *The Northernmost Ruins of the Globe*. Meddelelser om Grønland. Man & Society 29. Copenhagen, Sila & Danish Polar Centre.

Hoff, E. (1992). *Ekspeditioner. Grønland og Island*. Copenhagen, Fiskers Forlag.

Holtved, E. (1944). *Archaeological Investigations in the Thule district, I–II*. Meddelelser om Grønland 141 (1–2).

Holtved, E. (1954). *Archaeological Investigations in the Thule District, III: Nûgdlit and Comer's Midden*. Meddelelser om Grønland 146(3).

Inizian, M. L., M. Reduron-Ballinger, H. Roche, J. Tixier (1999). *Technology and Terminology of Knapped Stone*. Nanterre, CREP.

Jensen, J. F. (2003). 'Moskusoksevejen – en arktisk ørkenvandring'. In: G. Martens, J. F. Jensen, M. Meldgaard and H. Meltofte (eds.), *Peary Land*. Nuuk, Atuagkat, 147–173.

Knuth, E. (1952). 'An outline of the archaeology of Peary Land'. *Arctic* vol. 5, no. 1: 17–33.

Knuth, E. (1977). *Archaeology of Nares Strait I. Gammel Nûgdlît. A site with two paleo-eskimo levels in the Thule District, North Greenland*. Unpublished manuscript. Dronningens Håndbibliotek (Queen's Library), Copenhagen.

Knuth, E. (1977/78). 'The "Old Nudglit Culture" site at Nudglit Peninsula, Thule District, and the "Meso-Eskimo" site below it'. *Folk* 1977/78 19–20: 15–47.

Knuth, E. (1978). 'Grønlands tredelte forhistorie'. *Forskning i Grønland/Tusaat* 3/78: 7–22.

Meldgaard, J. (1952). 'A Paleo-Eskimo Culture in West Greenland'. *American Antiquity* 17(3): 222–230.

Madsen, B. (1992). 'Hamburgkulturens flintteknologi i Jels'. In: J. Holm and F. Reick (eds.), *Istidsjægere ved Jelssøerne*. Skrifter fra Museumsrådet for Sønderjyllands Amt 5. Haderslev, Haderslev Museum.

Pelegrin, J. (1990). 'Prehistoric Lithic Technology: Some aspects of research'. *Archaeological Review from Cambridge* vol. 9:1 (Technology in the humanities): 116–126.

Pelegrin, J. (1995). 'Technologie Lithique le Chattelperronien de Roc-De-Combe (Lot) et de La Côte (Dordogne)'. *Cahiers du Quarternaire* no. 20.

Pelegrin, J., C. Karlin et al. (1988). 'Chaîne opératoire: un outil pour le prehistorien'. In: J. Tixier (ed.), *Technologie Préhistorique. Notes et Monographies Techniques* no. 25: 55–62.

Rasmussen, K. (1919). *Grønland langs Polhavet. Udforskningen af Grønland fra Melvillebugten til Kap Morris Jesup: skildring af Den II. Thule-Ekspedition 1916–18.* Copenhagen, Gyldendalske Boghandel, Nordisk Forlag.

Rasmussen, K. (1921). *Grønland i tohundredaaret for Hans Egedes Landing.* Meddelelser om Grønland LX, 517–567.

Salomonsen, F. (1981). 'Fugle'. In: B. Muus, F. Salomonsen and C. Vibe, *Grønlands Fauna-Fisk-Fugle-Pattedyr.* Copenhagen, Gyldendal, 159–361.

Schledermann, P. (1980). 'Polynias and Prehistoric Settlement Patterns'. *Arctic* vol. 33, no. 2: 292–302.

Schledermann, P. (1990). *Crossroads to Greenland.* Calgary, University of Calgary.

Schledermann, P. and K. McCullough (1992). 'Crossroads Project 1992. Archaeological and Ethnographic Investigations in North Greenland'. Unpublished Report. The Arctic Institute of North America. The University of Calgary.

Stapert, D. and L. Johansen (1999). 'Flint and Pyrite: making fire in the Stone Age'. *Antiquity* 73: 765–777.

Steensby, H. P. (1910). *Contributions to the Ethnology and Anthropogeography of the Polar Eskimos.* Meddelelser om Grønland 34, 253–405.

Sørensen, M. (2006a). 'Teknologi og Tradition i Østarktis 2500 BC - 1200 AD. En dynamisk teknologisk undersøgelse af de litiske inventarer i de palæoeskimoiske traditioner'. Unpublished Ph.D. thesis, University of Copenhagen, Department of Archaeology.

Sørensen, M. (2006b). 'The Chaîne Opératoire Applied to Arctic Archaeology. Dynamics of Northern Societies'. In: J. Arneborg and B. Grønnow (eds.), *Proceedings from the Sila/Nabo conference, May 2004.* Copenhagen, 31–44.

Sørensen, M. (2006c). 'Teknologiske traditioner i Maglemosekulturen. En diakron analyse af maglemosekulturens flækkeindustri. Stenalderstudier. Tidlig mesolitiske jægere og samlere i Sydskandinavien. In: B. V. Eriksen (ed.), *Stenalderstudier. Tidligt mesolitiske jægere og samlere i Sydskandinavien.* Aarhus, Jutland Archaeological Society, 19–77.

Sørensen, M. (2011). *Technology and Tradition in the Eastern Arctic, 2500 BC–AD 1200: A Dynamical Technological Investigation of Lithic Inventories in the Palaeo-Eskimo Traditions.* Monographs on Greenland vol. 350. Copenhagen.

Sørensen, M. and C. Andreasen (2006). '"Geo-Ark 2003". Arkæologisk berejsning af: Wollaston Forland, Nordlige Clavering Ø, Sydspidsen af Kuhn Ø'. Report, SILA-Feltrapport nr. 23. Nationalmuseet København, Grønlands Nationalmuseum og Arkiv. Copenhagen.

Thostrup, C. B. (1911). *Ethnographic Description of the Eskimo Settlements and Stone Remains in North-East Greenland.* Meddelelser om Grønland no. 44.

Vibe, C. (1950). *The Marine Mammals and the Marine Fauna in the Thule District (Northwest Greenland) with observations on ice conditions in 1939–41.* Meddelelser om Grønland no. 150.

As of 2008 Museum Tusculanum Press has taken over the series
Monographs on Greenland | Meddelelser om Grønland.

MANUSCRIPTS SHOULD BE SENT TO
Museum Tusculanum Press
University of Copenhagen
126 Njalsgade, DK-2300 Copenhagen S
Denmark
info@mtp.dk | www.mtp.dk
Tel. +45 353 29109 | Fax +45 353 29113
VAT no.: 8876 8418
Guidelines for authors can be found at www.mtp.dk/MoG

ORDERS
Books can be purchased online at www.mtp.dk, via order@mtp.dk, through any of MTP's distributors in the US, UK, and France or via online retailers and major booksellers.
Museum Tusculanum Press bank details:
Amagerbanken, DK-2300 Copenhagen S
BIC: AMBK DK KK
IBAN: DK10 5202 0001 5151 08
More information at www.mtp.dk/MoG

ABOUT THE SERIES
Monographs on Greenland | Meddelelser om Grønland (ISSN 0025 6676) has published scientific results from all fields of research on Greenland since 1878. The series numbers more than 345 volumes comprising more than 1250 titles.
In 1979 Monographs on Greenland | Meddelelser om Grønland was developed into a tripartite series consisting of
Bioscience (ISSN 0106-1054)
Man & Society (ISSN 0106-1062)
Geoscience (ISSN 0106-1046)
Hence *Monographs on Greenland | Meddelelser om Grønland* was renumbered in 1979 ending with volume no. 206 and continued with volume no. 1 for each subseries. As of 2008 the original Monographs on Greenland | Meddelelser om Grønland numbering will be continued in addition to the subseries numbering. Further information about the series, including addresses of the scientific editors of the subseries can be found at
www.mtp.dk/MoG